Swing Trading

A Passive Income Guide with Strategies to Reach Financial Freedom Trading Stocks and Options

Gabriele Undig

Table of Contents

Chapter 1: Introduction of Swing Trading

Chapter 2: Swing Trading vs. Day Trading
    Potential Returns
    Varying Capital Requirements
    Time Difference
    Focus, Time, and Practice

Chapter 3: The Basics of Swing Trading Stocks and Options
    Identification of an Asset
    Visualize a Pathway
    Identify Your Strike Price
    Settle on the Date of Expiration
    Strategize Your Entry
    Trade
    Own Your Position

Chapter 4: How Swing Trading Strategy to Options Are Valid to Create a Passive Income Business
    Options Strategies
    Guides on How to Swing with Options Trading for Passive Income Generation
    Brokers to Help You Become Better at Swing Trading for Options

Chapter 5: Financial Instruments, Tools, and Platforms
    Financial Instruments

What to Consider During the Selection of Financial Instruments
The Five Major Financial Instruments
    Forex
    Stock Indices
    Equities
    Commodities
    Government Treasuries and Exchange-Traded Funds
Financial Instrument to Trade-In
Best Stock Trading Platforms for Buying Stocks
    Swing Trading with TD Ameritrade
    Ally Invest
    E-Trade
Best Stock Trading Tools for Backtesting and Technical Analysis
    Tickeron
    MarketSmith
    Tradingview
    Yewno Edge
    StockCharts

Chapter 6: Within the Technical Analysis Focus on Charting Basics, Indicator Tools and Patterns

The Basics of Technical Analysis
Assumptions in Technical Analysis
Utilization of Technical Analysis
Patterns and Indicators

Trend Lines in Technical Analysis
    Trend Lines Basics
    Support and Resistance
Chapter 7: Guiding Principles, Rules, and Strategies of Swing Trading
    Strategies and Rules of Swing Trading

Chapter 1: Introduction of Swing Trading

Swing trading can be described as a type of trading that involves holding trading positions for a varied period of several days or weeks. There are certain moments that a trader can hold his or her trading position for a period of months. Most of the fundamentalists love swing trading because they require several days or weeks for them to be able to execute their trades. There are reasonable amounts of profits that can be realized in the event an individual can be able to wait for a varied amount of days or weeks.

The reality of swing trading is that it sits in the middle of two forms of trading: trend trading and day trading. An individual performing day trading holds his or her trading position for a varied time of a couple of seconds but not exceeding a day, while trend trading involves the examination of long-term analysis of the trend in stocks or indexes. The next step would be a trader holding his or her position for a couple of weeks or months. A swing trader is characterized by holding the stocks being traded for several days or weeks. The common insight around day trading is that it is dependent on the oscillations experienced intra-week or intra-day.

Swing trading has the potential of being successful when an individual chooses the right stock to trade. The best forms of stocks that can be traded effectively are the large-cap stocks. These types of stocks are famous across major trades in financial markets. Large-cap stocks have the potential of swinging from high to low, broad extremes in the financial markets. This gives a trader the leverage to flow with the wind in a certain direction and later jump to the opposite side if there is a shift in the market.

The two market extremes are known as the bear and bull markets. Swing trading has the potential of being different in either of the two market conditions. Active stocks do not have the potential of exhibiting similar down and up oscillations in these two market extremes. The act is different compared to indexes, which tend to be relatively steady for a couple of weeks or months. The momentum of the market has the potential of carrying stocks in a certain direction irrespective of the bull or bearish market. The phenomenon is proof for an individual to trade in the direction of seeking long-term gains.

A person performing swing trade is advantaged in the event that the market goes nowhere, which means the moment the index prices rise and fall in a couple of days and the same phenomena repeat itself. The market is characterized by several months going by, and the original price values of stocks and indexes staying relatively the same. However, there are several ways an individual can be able to capture the gains in the market with these kinds of small margin shifts.

The usage of simple moving averages provides an individual with support and resistance levels in the market. They go ahead to making an individual have the clue of bearing and bulling patterns in the financial markets. They are points that signify if a swing trader can buy the stock. One the other hand, bulling and bearish points provide a trader with points where he or she can enter or exit the stocks.

A swing trader can go ahead using exponential moving averages (EMAs), which can be described as the variation experienced in simple moving averages. The technique places its utmost emphasis on the current data points. The exponential moving average has the potential of giving a swing trader a signal that is clear on the exit and entry points at a faster rate compared to moving averages. The crossover points of this technique is used by several traders in the time of entry and exit points.

There is a basic way that a crossover the system of the EMA can be designed. It can be put to focus on the nine, thirteen, or fifty periods of EMAs. The moment prices of moving averages being to be below is a depicting of bullish cross over. There are two factors that such a market wave would be able to bring. The situation might signify the upward trend that would be witnessed, and there would be a market reversal. A long entry would be portrayed when the signal crosses from the ninth point to the thirteenth point. However, the point is supposed to be above the thirteenth point or over the fiftieth mark.

The bearish crossovers are experienced in the event the markets when the market trends fall below the EMA values. The phenomenon signifies a potential market reversal that could occur. The situation is a perfect time for a swing trader to enter into a long position. A short entry position, also known as exiting of a long position, is executed in the event a trader sees the 9 EMA position being below thirteen. However, the thirteenth period is required to be below the fiftieth point.

It is a common knowledge that any person performing trading would aim to create profits. There is a certain way that is unique when a swing trader aims to make profits. He or she would try to exit the trade at close points, which are low or upper the channel line. The act is done without him or her being too precise. Certain markets are filled with strong directional trends. The markets subject a swing trader to wait for the channel to be depicted before him or her pulling out his or her profits. On the other hand, a trader can be able to pull his or her profit in a market that is weak. The action is possible if the market is not hit with directional trends. The profits in swing trading can be experienced with either intermediate or beginner traders.

Chapter 2: Swing Trading vs. Day Trading

The period stipulated for trading has a very adverse effect on strategy and profitability. This is with regard to the options a trader has settled. Day trading is commonly known for its traders opening and closing several positions in a span of a single trading day. On the other hand, swing traders are famous for their act of holding trading positions for a span of several days and weeks, and this can go ahead to several days. Taking a microscopic view, you will be able to realize that these two types of trading are different from their descriptions.

The two forms of active trading have the potential of suiting different traders depending on their preferences. The trader's preference can be as a result of capital available, psychology, available time, and the type of active market being traded. There are several fallacious ideologies that have been spread about the two types of trading. The argument is that either swing trading or day trading being better than the other. The fallacy is because swing trading or day trading will be preferred by a trader based on his or her personal circumstances.

There are several options provided in active markets that can make a trader fall in either of the two forms of trading.

Potential Returns

Day trading is prone to attracting a certain group of traders. The type of traders being referred to would be those who are in dire need of gains that compound rapidly. The best assumption that can be made would be that of a trader who is willing to risk 0.5 of his or her investment capital on every single execution of a trade. If a trader experiences loss, he or she will lose 0.5%. However, if a trader experiences gain in the financial markets, he or she would be able to gain 1% of the capital invested. The situation would be able to depict a risk-reward ration of 2:1, which is favorable for the trader's success.

The other assumption that can be made will be if this trader makes a gain of 50% from the trades he or she executes. If a trader can make close to six trades on a trading day, he or she would be able to make a 1.5% add on to his or her account. This would be an average gain on a single trading day after the deduction of trading fees. It would be intriguing and sound interesting to know what this trader has the potential of making in a year if he or she gains 1% of every trade execution. The findings are the trader has the potential of making over 200% in a variance of a year if the interests have not been compounded.

An individual is supposed to know the flip side concerning day trading. The numbers might sound pleasing to the eyes of a person, but pleasing results do not come as easy as it may seem. The market is set in a way that making doubles of gains has a similar result in moments you are a loser in the market. Making a gain of 50% of all the trades a person executes does not come easily. The issue one can be able to make speedy gains from day trading, but a trader can deplete his or her account at a rapid rate.

Swing trading is commonly known for accumulating losses and gains by a slow rate compared to day trading. However, this is not a fixed scenario because there are certain forms of swing trades that can make a trader accumulate losses and gains at a speedy rate. We can still use the assumption of swing trader using similar trading risk management strategies. The assumption goes ahead to having the thought of the trader risking 0.5% of his or her investment capital. The major aim of this trader is to make 1%-2% of his or her swing trades.

The assumption would be he or she is making 1.5% averagely from the winnable trades. On the other side, this trader loses 0.5% from every loss he or she incurs in the trades he or she loses. The trader has the potential of executing six trades to make a 50% gain. If this is the occurrence in a normal month, a swing trader has the potential of making 3% gain in his or her account. The occurrence of gaining 3% is realistic after the deductions of trading fees. The gains amount to 36% over the course of one year. The gains might seem interesting, but a swing trader has more potential gains at the end of the year.

These examples are meant to serve one major purpose. The function of these illustrations is to depict the difference between the two trading styles, which are day trading and swing trading. The alterations of the percentages value of the trades that have been won tend to have drastic effects on the potential of earnings. The figures referred to are those of the number of trades or average wins or losses.

The general rule is that day trading has high-profit potential, but the effect of profit levels is hugely felt by a trader with a small trading account. At the moment the account grows, a day trader is prone to having a hard task to utilize the entire amount in the account in an effective manner as there is a time limit for day trading since it is characterized by short-term trades during the day. On the other hand, day traders can find their capital declining as the level of capital they have increased. Their gain per dollar might still be able to increase their returns. It is because gaining 5% on $1,000,000 investment will bring a return of $100,000, which is 20% of $1,000,000. The chances of a swing trader to having such a return investment are very minimal.

Varying Capital Requirements

The capital requirement differs depending on the type of market that an individual is trading in. There are several factors that make day trading and swing trading have varied capital requirements. Starting capital will be deferent when trading either in the futures, stock, or the foreign exchange markets.

Day trading in the stock in the US financial market would be a good depiction. The market requires an individual performing day trading to have a minimum of $25,000. There are no legal minimums for a trader who is performing swing trading on stocks. However, a swing trader is advised to have a minimum of $10,000 in their account. However, a person performing swing trading is encouraged to have a minimum capital of $20,000 to make his or her swing trades to be more viable. The stipulated will help him or her to draw a good income from his or her trades.

The other financial market in the US economy would be the Foreign Exchange market. There are no minimum legal requirements when it comes to this form of financial instrument. The minimum recommendation for an individual interested in performing day trading is $500. However, having $1,000 would prove to have viable returns from the trades that will be executed. Swing trading in the forex market will have a trader prepare to invest close to $1,500 and more. The amount would prove to be very advantageous because a trader will be enabled to enter a few trading positions at a single time with this amount.

Day trading futures in the US financial market also has several capital requirements that are different. A trader seeking to day trade is advised to start his or her investment with an amount of $5,000 to $7,500. It would also be advantageous to the trader in the event he or she has the potential to invest more capital in this form of active trading. These amounts are also dependable with the kind of futures that are being traded. There are certain features that require huge capital investment when being traded when compared to others. There are features that require minimal capital investment to be traded. These contracts include the likes of micro-contracts.

Swing trading features has its own different capital requirement in the US financial markets. A trader interested in this ventured is advised to have at least an investment capital of $10,000. However, such a trader is advised to invest an amount of $20,000 or more. The amount being invested is always dependent on the margin prerequisites of a precise future being trade.

Time Difference

The factual truth is that both day trading and swing trading require time from a trader. However, a trader must keep in mind that day trading takes more time compared to swing trading. An individual performing day trading is required to spend at least two hours performing his or her tasks in a day. The minimum spent on a computer can increase depending on the time an individual spends on a computer. The time can increase to spending close to five to four hours on a computer. The reason for the additional time is preparation for trading that is done through reading and analyzing the trading charts. The investment of a day trader can go up if he or she trades for more hours in a day. The major reason for increased investments would be because of the act would be a full-time job.

Swing trading has the potential of taking less time compared to day trading. For example, a swing trader executing his or her trades based on the daily charts. This trader would be in a position to be able to find new trading positions and update the current position at an estimated time of forty-five minutes in one night. The time spent is very minimal because this kind of trader would not be subjected to execute his or her trades daily.

There are certain famous swing traders that are taking trades having the potential lasting a week or several months. It brings also brings a new outlook on the amount of time spent to execute swing trades. Such type of swing trader only requires a single day in a week to execute his or her trades. The new outlook would be the usage of one hour on a single day of a week. The action is performed in a single day is not restricted to every night.

There are moments trader does day trading in moments the markets are open and very active. There are certain moments during the day that are very favorable for an individual who is performing day trading. The favorable moments have the potential of limiting day trading. If a trader finds it difficult to perform day trading during these moments, he or she is advised to shift and perform swing trading as the better option. The reason is a swing trader has the leverage of looking trade order and place the trade at any time of the day. The act of placing trades in swing trading can be done even if the markets have been closed.

There is a common occurrence known as a second-to-second shift in the prices of underlying assets. The phenomenon rarely affects swing trader because these traders tend to look at the bigger picture. The act involves analyzing daily charts and placing their trades after the market closes still works perfectly for them. On the other hand, day trading involves capturing the gains from second-to-second shifts that are experienced in the market. The implication makes a day trader be present when these shifts are being experienced.

Focus, Time, and Practice

There are certain convergent points between these two forms of trading, where both require an individual to have a deep level of knowledge. A trader who has a deep level of knowledge has the best potential of making huge gains, but the knowledge being referred to do not necessarily mean being book smart. Success in trading would result if a trader can find viable strategies. The technique is settled upon as supposed to be able to give an individual an advantage in making profits or gains in his or her trades.

There are two major factors that can make an individual have an easy time when it comes to generating profits. A trader is supposed to have a piece of deep knowledge about the kind of market he or she is investing in and the type of profitable strategy he or she is settling. However, there are several factors that can contribute to an individual's success. The prices of several assets tend to fluctuate every day; this means that a trader is supposed to be able to adapt to several market conditions given the type of strategy he or she is using.

The situation of fluctuating market prices of assets can prove to be a tricky situation as it is a difficult task to find a market strategy that can be able to always make a trader gain from the market constantly. However, this is not supposed to be the end for an individual who is a beginner. There are several ways that have been developed to overcome this situation. The famous way involves the development of several trading demos prior to the execution of a trade in a demo account. One would be advantaged since it reduces risk factors.

The idea to settle for either day trading or swing trading is also determined by the personality of a person. There are huge amounts of stress when it comes to day trading. The process of day trading also requires a trader to be disciplined and have high levels of focus for a very long time. People who have fast reflexes are favored with this kind of trading. It is common to find these kinds of people liking games such as poker or video games.

Swing trading, on the other hand, occurs at a very slow pace. There is a long time-lapse taken when an individual enters and exits trading positions. The process also has high levels of stress that come with trading and requires an individual to be focused too. The level of patience and disciple involved in this kind of trading is immense. However, it does not require an individual to have a strained level of focus, unlike day trading. Day trading is also not concerned with how fast an individual is since trades can be executed if the market closes.

Chapter 3: The Basics of Swing Trading Stocks and Options

From the previous chapters, we have already gathered what swing trading entails, and we have looked at the comparison between swing trading and day trading. With this in mind, we have gathered the strengths and weaknesses that lie with each aspect. This chapter is keen to focus on the basics of swing trading and the options available for a swing trader. We are going to look at how one may institute swing trading and hold on to it until it matures. With swing trading, traders at all levels of trading may learn how to indulge. The main element considered in swing trading is the relative strength index, often denoted as RSI. The purpose of this particular index is to provide for the information as to when market movements will be overdone. This information is quite crucial because it is a ripe indicator of when to venture into the market. The indication is that the market is ripe for correction; thus, it means that the market is shifting to another direction. In most forms of trading, the turning point is often the ripest point to enter into trade as there will be many amateurs in the market which makes it easy for exploitation, and if the price was on a fall, the opposite direction will arise and will exceed a point when it reaches the highest point.

As we have already gathered in the previous chapters, swing trading is one of the forms of active trading. Swing traders tend to take a long-term approach towards trade as compared to other normal day traders or scalper traders. The duration that a swing trader takes in business is, however, lesser as compared to a trend trader. Strategic swing traders opt to trade at night time as it functions when day traders have closed trading. The advantage of this type of trading is that purchased options tend to have a downside risk that is controlled, which means it is limited. That is why it is safer for them to run at night. For individuals who are trading small accounts, it is more reliable for them to assume swing trading. Traders with small accounts can venture into big accounts without necessarily having to spend big time. Swing trading is friendly to traders with small accounts because you do not necessarily need to have much capital. It has already been simplified; all you need to do is to purchase an option and wait on it until it matures.

Swing trading carries with it a bag of goodies that are not limited to huge profit potential. There is no businessman or woman for that sake that would engage in any business without a view of profit. You ought to adopt a step-by-step approach that will enable you to cover all aspects synchronically. Your radar will be focused on picking up the right kind of stock, but before anything else, you will have to analyze the market environment with the help of various tools of analysis. The settling on your strike price is what will follow. When you are home with your strike price, you will then shift your focus to the expiration date and then focus on racing against time.

When we talk about an option in swing trading, this is a derivative instrument that can be referred to financially. This option has an effect of providing its holder the leeway to participate in business in return for a premium which may come as payment. One characteristic of the financial markets is that it has an exercise or strike price. This type of price is used in contemplating the levels at which the buyer can dispose the financial asset. The striking factor about options is that they come with a date of expiration at which the option ceases to exist. A group of traders known as options traders has a variety of option strategies that they use in trading. These types of options traders have an implication where the trader can decide to sell one particular option to observe what lies beneath the asset.

Payoff profiles are a type of graph used by the particular traders to project and see what the venture tends to offer. This is often calculated upon the expiration date of that particular option and carried out on a range of underlying markets. The graph below is an indication of what happens in this type of trading.

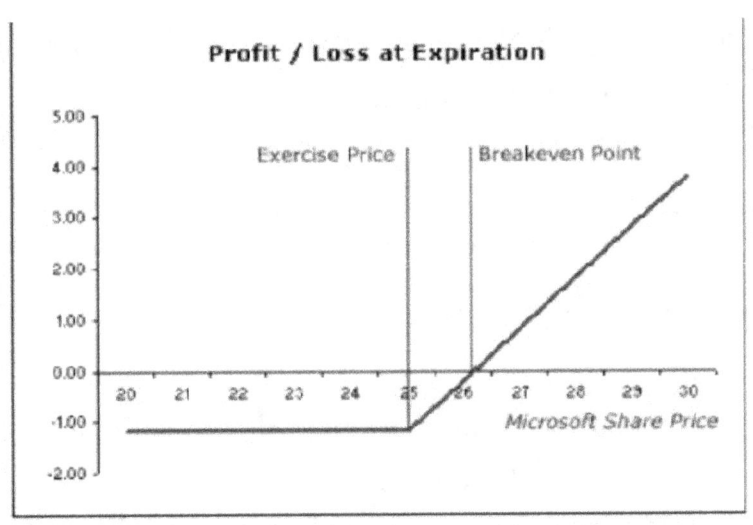

Option payoff profile for a $25 call on Microsoft shares. Source: OptionTradingTips.com

The graph has a line that shows how profit is gained just at the expiration date. This will only take place if the market is overwhelming enough to surpass the break-even point. The graph has not indicated however that a buyer can be able to achieve profit before the expiration date. This will only happen if the buyer sold the position at an amount that is higher than the one he or she acquired it for. Any trader's objective is to achieve profit through the use of various curves that work in your favor. Swing trading is not left aside as it works to achieve profit by considering the options available.

It is less subtle to decode the various strategies and options that may be used in swing trading and this is what makes it easy for many people to engage in it. A number of steps that can be used to ensure an individual is taking part in swing trading in the right way include the simplest steps. This may include the purchase of a call or put.

Identification of an Asset

When it comes to option trading, the initial step is to select an asset and dwell on it. This asset should be linked to the opportunity of trading that has been selected too. To ensure that you achieve a market that best works for you, you need to consider the fact that observing several asset markets will work for you. Observing does not only refer to the mere outlook. With observation, one would be inclined to monitor several assets and take note of their movements in terms of shifts. When you are in search of a market, you ought to be keen enough to know you are taking note of correction meaning you are considerate of the fact that the market will change. As mentioned earlier, this is the ripe point of entry. The determinants of these points of correction are often a momentum indicator which can be the RSI. These momentum indicators operate on a principle of overbought and oversold, suggesting that the market is overbought when it is over seventy and oversold when it is under thirty.

Simply put, you should search to dispose of your position when its indicator is over seventy and seek to acquire a position when its indicator is below thirty. More patient swing traders have achieved through waiting until they visualize an indicator known as the Price-RSI divergence, a type of signal that indicates that a price ought to have made a significant move, for instance, hitting a major shift towards a high. When this happens, and the RSI fails to do so, it is what is known as a price divergence. With this signal at hand, you can note that the price is above is in the process of achieving imminent correction.

Visualize a Pathway

After you have settled on a particular market, you have observed the various markets by the use of various tools which are not limited to fundamental and technical analysis. The following procedure is to search for a trading opportunity that is good enough to provide you with the amount of profit projection that you require. This may be in the ratio of 2 or 1. After you have achieved this, the following steps will entail that you observe a market directionally, which means looking at the destination of the market versus time. If the market will assume a rise, you are taking the rise to your advantage. By the use of a call option, one would consider adopting a long-term relationship with the underlying asset to make sure that he or she is maximizing the profits. One of the key factors that traders observe when indulging in this form of trade is upside and downside risk. An asset that has a limited upside potential is one that is rising and rising; it will go top-notch if given time. The factor of having a limited downside risk is present so that the price of the asset does not fall below its limits. If your option is to influence the market when it is going to fall, you will do this on a short-term basis so that you are maximizing on the short-term profits before they are used up. The idea is to maintain the downside risk which is limited and the upside risk which is unlimited.

Below is an example of an option to pay off an important profile when it comes to identifying the projected expiration date of a particular asset. This way, you can project on how the price will fair in the market. The chart shows how losses are reduced to a minimum. This is relative to the premiums paid. Losses will only be calculated when your projection turns out to be incorrect. When your projection turns out to be correct, you will encounter profits that will be calculated as when the price hits past the break-even point. The gains will automatically overwhelm the amount of premium that has been paid.

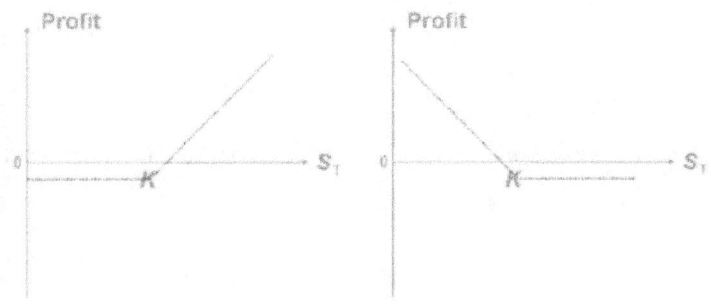

Call and put option payoff profiles with a strike price of K. Source: Surlytrader.com

Identify Your Strike Price

In options trading, also referred to as swing trading, the strike price of an asset is relevant when it comes to determination of that particular last price. The market is the first observant of the strike price, and when it does so and the market is attracted, the asset will be easily disposed. The option is valued against time because with each dawn, the price keeps escalating. The amount of duration in which an option has until its expiration is what will count a lot when it comes to valuation. The more time an asset has until its expiration, the more expensive that particular asset is. The better positioned a strike price is in relation to the market is what causes an option to be in the money (ITM), a phrase which means that the option has an intrinsic value which makes it be the same as the discrepancy that lies between the market price that is in existence and the strike price itself.

When the strike price of a particular option is at the market (ATM), the price of an option relates to the market price. The last form is when the price of an option is lower than what is currently in the market, then the price is said to be out of the market (OTM). When you look at OTM and ATM with an in-depth view, you find that both of them tend to lack intrinsic value. This means that the market is most likely to overwhelm them. It is a nature of swing traders that their view is to profit from shifts in the short-term but profitable market. With a long-term view of the market, swing traders will look to profit from shifts in the anticipated market. If they make it succeed, then the profit is tremendous, but if they fail, the loss also takes a toll on them. Most swing traders would anticipate these shifts over time. The onset of these particular traders would be to choose on an OTM, which they have the hopes that it will have a drastic move towards ITM.

With options, they are encompassed with intrinsic value as we have seen in the ITM and also with time value because you are no longer in a position to sell your asset when the time value expires. The time factor gives swing traders regret that comes from the desire to go back and purchase a position at the time when its ability to making profit was still ripe and also when the time value of the option was higher. Time value enhances the price of an option.

Settle on the Date of Expiration

With an expiration date in mind, you can know the limits that you are going to work with, so you are not going to move blindly. You have a vision of how long you are going to take to arrive at your destination, and with this in mind, you will know how to manipulate the market so you arrive at your objective. Depending on how you have structured your move, you settle on either a long-term or short-term venture. As earlier mentioned, there are various moves in the market in which a swing trader can consider using to thrive.

In the mind of a swing trader, there exist various thoughts whereby you do not want to engage in a venture that has an earlier expiration date and thus seeing you out of the market before you can make any profit, as well as engaging yourself in a long-term adventure whereby you are going to be in the wait for quite long which may lead to incurring further costs that are quite higher than what you had projected. For more experienced swing traders, they play within the time jurisdiction of one month or so. With a month, you can relatively project the direction in which the option is taking. You need to visualize the pathway as earlier mentioned because this is what brings about relativity in what you are engaging in. Failure to observe the market will see to it that you are moving in a manner that is disadvantageous to yourself.

When you are speculating about the expiration date, the underlying factors of asset type should be kept in mind. The expiration date is what gives the option its time value which is also its life. Take a scenario where you have selected an expiration date for a particular asset that will not make it to the expiration date. This leads to losses accruing from all directions. An expiration date is a key element that ought to be considered during the whole process of swing trading. Take the example of a time bomb waiting to designate, and the only time you have for escape has expired.

Strategize Your Entry

With knowledge of technical analysis, you will find out that the entries to a particular trade often follow a particular direction. An initial step for a swing trader is to identify the trend that is prevailing. Once you have gathered this, then you can follow through your path. The identification of a trend is directly related to the asset. It is only after you identify an asset is when you will find out the direction that the asset is taking, which is known as its trend. Each asset has a discrepant trend which enables traders to make profit as a result of their various shifts and movements. The observation of the desired asset throughout its trend is what leads to an asset forming an entry point. The attention of many swing traders while trading would be drawn towards various shifts, for instance, a corrective pullback is what arouses them. The RSI is the main indicator here that will be observed to bring about a showcase of whether the price is in the back form or is in present form. We have earlier seen the implications of oversold and overbought. This means that the observance of the RSI levels is what will influence various buyers to settle on a particular option. Normally, you find that most traders would want to start low and work themselves through the time value for them to achieve profit, which mainly relates to long-term traders. As for short-term traders, they would simply anticipate the short term changes in the price.

When the particular pullback of an option seems to be in the direction where it is in the process of its momentum diminishing, this will be signaled by the RSI levels of oversold and overbought, clearly distinguishing these zones, then this seems like the right time that one would consider to get into the market.

Trade

You had already implemented a trading plan in place, and once you can achieve this, then you can work according to your trading plan. You have had time throughout the technical and fundamental analysis to arrive at an option that is favorable to you. With this in mind, you need to execute your plan in the best way possible to see to it that you are making a profit. For instance, an individual may choose to purchase an OTM option which is particularly above the market. This particular trader will then anticipate a downfall or a trend that is headed towards the floor.

How you trade is almost as directly linked as where you carry out your trade. There are various factors that come with trading in swing, for instance, the issue of costs and fees. For a frequent swing trader, the understanding of this is key as you would be inclined to settling on a particular broker that is right for you. This broker will ensure that you have the best deals when it comes to costs and will also keep updating you on the shifts in the market. Brokers are a crucial factor when it comes to trading in swing because you will need them when it comes to various issues. There are various brokers available upon which a swing trader may choose on. In execution of the trade, you ought to remember that you have a plan in which you need to follow through.

Own Your Position

You can trade with the help of your broker and the projected time of entry. When have already traded, as the laws of swing trade suggest, you will have acquired a position. This position comes with profit or loss. The venture is risky although you are protected from adverse risk. You engaged trade through the process of purchase of an option, and by this fact alone, your downward risk will be limited to the amount of premium you have. The amount of premium that an individual has is dependent on the position that an individual decided to acquire. The amount paid in acquisition of the position is the premium. With this in mind, you need to consider the underlying market.

Take an instance where an individual purchased an option when it was at its OTM. The individual patiently waits until the option hits its strike price and it is at its ATM. The strike price of an option is one of the key determinants of the success of that particular option. When the strike price of an option is high, it means there are high chances of the option picking up a high price, and vice versa. Hitting a strike price for an option means that the option has achieved the best price that it could have in the market. When the time value of an option increases, it also has the same effect on the premium. The premium of an option is what sits as the value of an option in case it backslides and it is on the downward trend. The higher the premium, the higher the value of your option. The time value should never be underestimated because it is only through time that you can incur profit or loss.

As the dawn of a new day is appreciated, your time value tends to decrease because this is a step towards your expiration date. The race against time decay is one that ought not to be looked down upon because time decay catches up with every aspect of life. Your venture in the option should be swift so that time is in your favor. Potential gains will always be your arousal because anything that goes into the bag is a gain. With the view on time, a swing trader will be attentive enough to know when to sell back his position. This should be done at the earliest time possible as failure of this will lead to time decay eating up on this swing trader. You may have arrived at a down road and the way you visualize your plan, you can know that you are not likely to make it to your destination. This way, you need to take a strategic look back. This will often involve that you dispose your option to go back in time and try to reconsider your options and recreate your plan.

The selling back of your position is often premised on the fact that you thought your market would shift but failed to do so. This is often short-term anticipation which, when it failed to mature, you had to reconsider your options. In a bid to sell back your position, you can consider doing a trade in the rollout or executing a calendar spread. You can use the same strike to purchase a long-term position in the market. The strike price of the short-term position you acquired and that of the long-term position ought to go hand in hand. With this in place, you are shielded from sharp losses that come as a result of sudden shifts in the market. The expiration date is often one of the factors that make it subtle for swing traders to trade because, just as your trend was about to assume direction the right, then you are hit with an uncertain curve that will lead to you contemplating about selling back. The merit that comes with selling back is that you are given time to gradually grow yourself through the limits and to make sure that you achieve once more. This is almost felt like a second chance towards trading.

Chapter 4: How Swing Trading Strategy to Options Are Valid to Create a Passive Income Business

When we think of passive income, we think entrepreneurs. But that does not tell the whole story. Passive income refers to regular income that comes from a place other than where you are employed or contracted. To build a site where you earn steady passive income, you need to put a lot of work upfront before you get to the point where you can make money regularly.

In swing trading, when you put money into options or stocks, you will then hold and wait for the right trade entry time, then execute your trade.

When you choose options trading in your swing trading venture, you could potentially earn high returns. It also has various strategies that would make it a less risky investment than stocks trading. But, generally, when you choose market trading, you are putting yourself up to risks through and through.

When you trade options, you, as the option buyer, have the opportunity to sell or buy the stock at a given premium. However, before we look at those, we give you a brief glimpse into the strategies that make up the options trading. Most of these will need you to take your time, but as we learn, the returns offer you an endless possibility of gains.

Before we look at how to swing strategies options are valid, let us look at some of the strategies when swing trading in options.

Options Strategies

Options trading is more complicated than stocks trading, which is vital to learn about strategies that you will need to use when you venture to the options market.

Long Call and Long Put. These two strategies are necessary and are slightly more straightforward when you want to trade options.

The long call involves the trader purchasing one or more call options with the bet that they will rise beyond the strike rate by the expiration date. The risk here is at a low, but it will need the trader to be bullish about the market even when they remain less sure about the direction the move will go.

In long put, the trader put their money in one or more options and puts their bet on the stocks going below the strike price by the day of expiry. In this type of trading, the market view then is bearish with the profit potential being unlimited and the risks being premium paid. This type of trading works in such a way that you get both limited gains and limited losses.

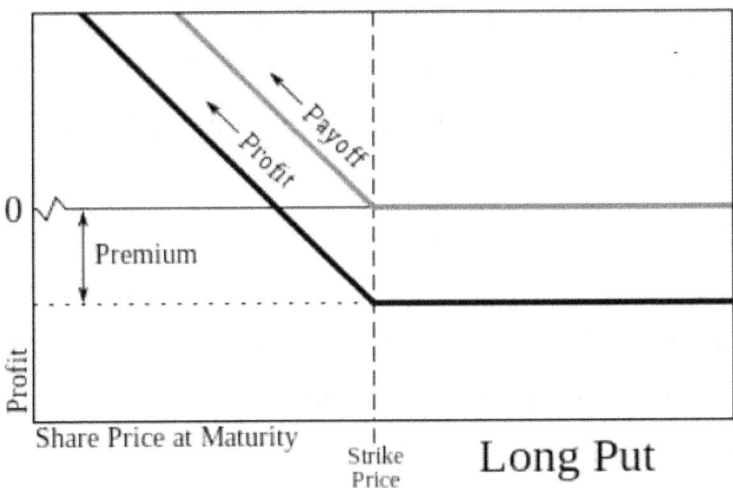

The long put diagram is showing us how a trader puts money in dropping market prices, and then makes profits when the prices drop beyond his or her stated values.

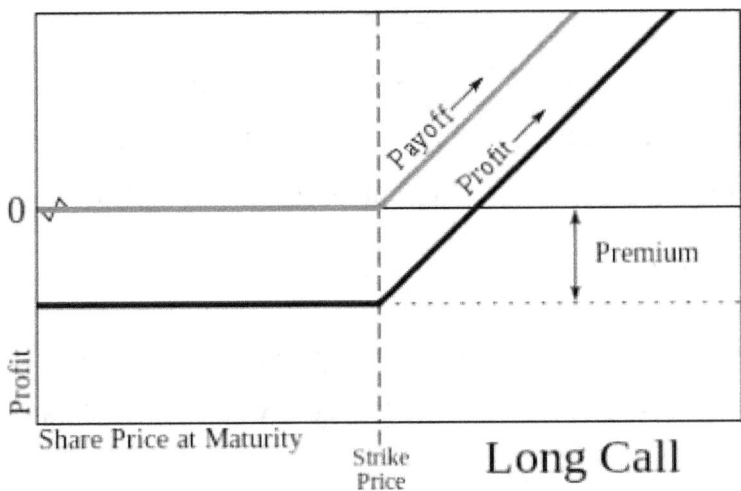

As we see in the long call diagram, the payoff and profits rise beyond the strike price while you pay the premium from the strike price and profit intersection. You walk away with maximum benefits once you sell your assets above the strike rate.

Protective Collar. From the name, this type of option strategy is meant to be neutral, thus, you protect yourself if the stocks fall. However, you get to sell your long shares and the strike rate of a short call.

This type of options strategy will give you high returns, with your profit being the distance between the prevailing market price and the call strike price. This protective put is when, let's say, you hold long 100 shares at a company for $45 in January, but then the options rise to about $80 as of March that year. As an investor, you could for a protective collar for yourself by trading part of your shares at a $100 call while also buying options in the same company at $75. When you do this, you will then not trade below $75 while still having the opportunities to sell them at $100.

Thus, you have the distance between the prevailing market price ($80) and the call strike price ($100), giving you potential gains of $20.

Protective Put. This type of trading is bearish, with the trader choosing to see the stocks as likely to decline. This strategy would involve buying a put when you are in the long stock. To purchase this put, you will need to do so when the market is still on the rise so that you ensure that you keep your payoff at a level.

Long Call Butterfly Spread. This is where the trader combines a bullish approach and bearish approach to trading. This situation means that they then have a strike price at three different places.

A trader will often do this when their analysis gives them the impression that there will not be many movements within the market by the date of expiration.

So, in this strategy, you purchase the options at a low strike rate, then selling two on the money options and then buying one more in the call option.

This option of trading will need you to have purchased both the long call and long put, which offer you the two options in this trading, so that you may know how to go about it. Do not use this strategy as your first, as it may lead to considerable losses. As we have seen, options trading is much safer than stocks trading. You have a high likelihood of profits here than in stocks. Take advantage and learn first.

Credit Spreads. In this strategy, you get to sell one put, but then immediately buy another one so that you can mitigate against losses. Here, you will find that you will get to limit the profits that you will earn, but it is all is for the best since you do not get to suffer losses. Losses are much more devastating to your pockets than additional money that was never in your pocket from the start.

So, when you make the trade-off for huge profits with reducing losses and making small gains, you will be able to handle the losses you suffer without much personal loss. This type of strategy acts as an insurance policy that will work out for you when you know how to make your moves.

Naked Puts. A naked put is a strategy where you sell when the stock price is higher than the put strike rate. In trading terms, they call it an out-of-the-money approach. Since you sell with stock prices higher than strike rate, you will collect a cash premium, which will be your profits, regardless of the circumstances.

Having looked at the strategies below, we give you guides on how you will then go about the swing trading with options trading so that you grow your passive income business.

Guides on How to Swing with Options Trading for Passive Income Generation

Select an Asset. To begin trading, you will need to identify which assets you want to trade-in. You should have identified a trading opportunity in this asset option, or else, you might find yourself holding without finding the right value to trade your options.

To identify which assets you want to trade in, identify the market's relative strength indicator (RSI), which is what will tell you if the market is due for a correction. A market due for correction will experience the right uptrends and downtrends that are critical when you are looking to trade in the short term, as with swing trading.

So, to make the best choice, always ensure that you make several different assessments of different markets, rather than focus on one or two. You will need to know which markets have the right level of being overbought (RSI value above 70) or being oversold (RSI appreciate is below 30).

47

When you sell with the market RSI values are above 70 and buy when they are below 30, then you stand a better chance of making profits. You could boost your analysis by using the price RSI divergence, which is the situation where the price makes a very extreme move that the RSI fails to capture. When you see this happen, that market might be ready for a correction. As we have seen, the stock market will always operate within a given range, with the low and high prices oscillating between known figures and within acceptable ranges. However, an extreme drop or rise in price is an excellent indicator that the market may be ready for a correction.

The extreme market movements are often due to several prevailing factors, such as the political climate of the country as well as new strategies introduced in the market. But when you trade, you gain the knowledge that markets will not stay in the extremes for long and that, with time, it will correct itself. This correction will result in a series of uptrends and downtrends, which is a perfect opportunity for you to then identify the options that you analyze and conclude they show maximum potential.

Know the Direction. In options trading, we have two options, as we saw in the strategies above: the call option and the put option.

So, once you have identified the asset you want to trade-in and have the technical or fundamental analysis in place, you will then choose a trading option. This option will give you better odds when you risk higher, which means that the asset should reward you twice the risk you put in. So, how would you use a call or options strategy?

When you make your analysis and find that the market is going to rise, then you will make the call option. This analysis will allow you to go long as it has excellent profit potential like we saw earlier in the strategies, as well as limiting your losses. This view is the bullish market view, and what you will be putting to use here will be the long call strategy.

However, when you view that the market is going to drop, you will then use the put action to pay so that you go short, all with the same reduced risks and yet, maintaining high-income potential, which is the long put strategy.

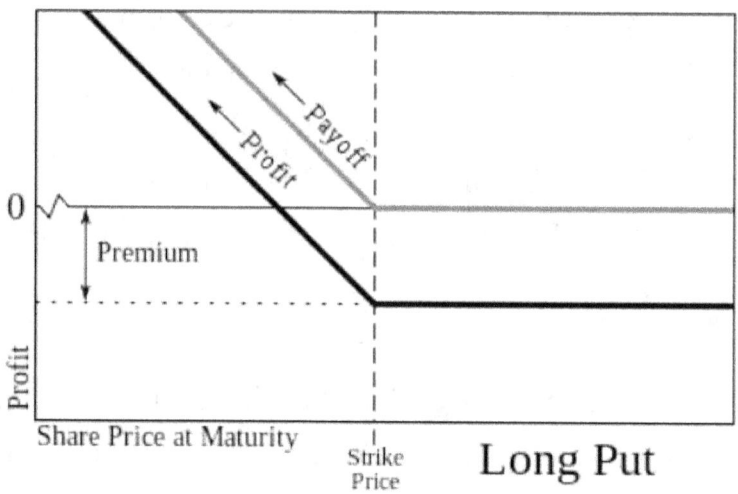

Long Put

The above is a diagram of the put action. When we look at it, we see that your losses will be limited to the premium below the profit potential. Thus, your risks are below your gains. So, if you made a wrong assumption about the market, you will suffer little losses. However, when you do make the right analysis, and when your assumption comes through right, you will find yourself staring at unlimited profits.

Strike Price. In options trading, your strike price is a way that helps you find the price of the asset. When this price is encouraging than the prevailing price in the market of the assets, there will then be a high cost on the option. When the end of the option with that strike is further ahead, your options increases in value too. This situation is said to then be 'in the money' (ITM). Meanwhile, there is a situation where the prices are much closer to each other (strike closer to market price). If your price is below the prevailing market price, then you are 'out of the money' (OTM).

When you are trading options where the strike rate is higher than the market rate, then, your choices have what traders call 'intrinsic value'. When there is a gainful advantage between the market price and strike value, that is when intrinsic value applies. Thus, when you are at the money or out of the capital, your options do not have intrinsic value.

Since you are looking to gain within a relatively short period, chose to buy OTM that your analysis reveals will go ITM in a relatively short time. When you sell the options once it hits the ITM value, you are keeping within the time value decay, which is when the options no longer have intrinsic value, the closer it inches to the expiration date. Thus, when an opportunity to trade ITM sooner presents itself, you take it with open arms.

Decide on Expiration Date. When you decide to choose your expiration date, you should keep in mind what your analysis of the market reveals about the time it will take the option to reach your objective. When you make these considerations, you will give yourself the time to think through. So, you will make the option short-term if you feel that you will hit the ITM faster, or you could choose the long-term if you think the opposite is exact. However, since we are still in swing trading, even when you want the long-term option, you will always bear in mind that you still desire to make your income within a relatively short period.

So, in this case, you will need to balance delicately between a short-term option and a long-term trade. You do not want to get caught in a situation where you set the expiration date too soon, leading to early expiry and thus losses. Neither will you want to have an expiration date that is too far into the future as this will also increase costs as it will put a dent into your pockets.

Entry Time. To know what time you need to make your entry, you will need all the tools of the technical analysis.

When you swing trade, you will realize that you will trade through the corrections of the market, as we saw in the first step where you are selecting an asset. If not, then you can always choose to make the trade with trends. First, you buck the trend, and then you follow the pattern. In given circumstances, trading against trends will need you to be thoroughly well-informed on how to follow the direction first. When you learn then to identify trends and track them, you gain a better understanding of how the corrections happen. You will know what circumstances lead to the revisions, leading to you then, knowing how you can buck the trend then.

So, once you identify a trend in your chosen asset option, you will then look for the corrective action so that you can find a position where the trend is going. When you see that the corrective action seems to have lost momentum, as you will see from the RSI figures, you will then make your entry. Then, you wait for the corrective measures to gain momentum then so that you can then trade.

Execute Your Trade. Once your time has come, you will then make your move according to how you planned.

As you make your trade, you will need to maintain your broker, as the place where you deal is as important as how you will go about it.

Beware of Your Position. Once you move in to trade, you then need to remain aware of your position in the trade. While the premium you paid for will mitigate against any potential losses, you will still need to keep your eyes on the underlying market. This keenness is so that you know when you will need to adjust your expiration date or to opt-out of a deal altogether.

Monitoring the position will allow you to pan the market and identify if you run the risk of not making profits as the expiry date nears. Thus, you will know when to sell your options that are nearing their expiration date so that you can purchase assets for a longer time at the same strike rate. This sale is what traders call executing a calendar spread or roll out trade.

When you remain in the know about your position, you avoid excessive time decay, which will limit your potential gains as the value of the asset decreases.

We have looked at the situations and strategies that you will need when you begin to trade options. Now, we then give you a choice of brokers that will help you navigate your way through the trading world. Having a good broker will often be the difference between you having a gain or a loss. With a basic understanding of the market, but a good broker guiding you, you will make the right moves and find yourself making the profits without much struggle.

Below, we give you a detailed look into some of the best brokers for swing trading. These brokers have a particular focus on options trading.

Brokers to Help You Become Better at Swing Trading for Options

Ally Invest. This trading platform will help you keep your option trading costs low while ensuring that you have the right tools to maximize your profits then.

Because of its low fees, this broker platform is best for beginners who are just making their maiden forays into the options market. However, it is one broker that you can use through the ranks. It has a standard pricing start at $4.95, with $0.65 on every contract. The higher you trade, the lower the feels drops. If you begin to make about 30 trades, you will then pay a fee of $3.95, with $0.50 per contract.

Gatsby. Gatsby is a user-friendly app for many young people, meaning that it will be great for you as a beginner. This broker manages to merge many different resources and expertise, ensuring that you have the chance to make better use of the lessons that you will learn.

This broker gives no commissions, meaning that once you sign up, you will have the option to begin trading right away. Because it is a broker that the founders aimed at your population, you have the opportunity of interacting with other brokers. They will ensure that, as a new trader, you do not get lost through the analysis. You aim to gain a better understanding of the trade market soon enough so that you can begin your passive income business. Having access to several experts then will be beneficial for you to earn your extra income.

However, the market analysis and research that you will find here will be minimal and may not be conclusive enough on its own.

E* Trade. This broker has a user-friendly desktop, as well as a mobile interface. It is one of the most detailed trading brokers that you can find, boasting of a well-researched database. This comprehensive information base makes it perfect for you even when you are a seasoned trader.

Because of its detail, you will find it easier to use when you have your market research in place and know what to look. It has tools for education and guidance that you will find useful when you begin to use it. The E*Trader also offers you complete banking services, meaning that you will quickly transfer your money from your bank account to the platform and back.

However, that said, because of its complicated nature, the E*Trader has a very high commission, beginning at $ 6.95 for less than 30 trades, while that figure drops to $4.95 when it is for trades above 30.

TD Ameritrade. This broker gets us right off the bat with the fact that you can make trades with a minimum of $0 in your account. This broker has a straightforward user interface, which means that you will navigate through it easily as a beginner.

What makes TD Ameritrade stand out more is that you get the option to trade virtually. This feature means that you will not need to put your real money at risk as you make the virtual trade your way of practicing. You also get customer service round the clock. You also have access to several classes and learning tools.

However, it has high commissions ($6.95), which might be discouraging for new traders. There is also the fact that it may be more friendly to traders who have done it for a while though it will not take long for you to get used to it.

Fidelity Investment. One significant advantage of Fidelity is that you will get loads of free research and data on its platform. Through a web of more than 20 credible sources, Fidelity gives the beginner all they need at no cost and in a way that they will find useful without feeling saturated by information.

Fidelity has low commission fees, starting at $4.95 per trade as well as $0.65 per contract. The broker also has free online classes as well as webinars, allowing new traders to gain information without having to spend more than they need or have.

Its vast database might make it intimidating for beginners, but this is mitigated with access to customer care round the clock.

However, all this for the relatively low commission seems like a reasonable trade-off.

Tastyworks. This trading site is best known for its low-commission as well as no charge when it comes to closing trade fees on futures, stocks, options for inventory, and options for the future.

With no charge in your closing trade, the commission for the first trade is varied, coming in at between $1 and $5 per contract. Tastyworks might have a little more charges that might accumulate when you begin to trade, so you will need to keep an eye on your moves within the app.

However, this broker allows you to open three different trading platforms; individual, entity, and joint. It also gives you tools and options to make better decisions on your choices. It is also fast in executing deals, all while keeping the costs low.

However, it has limited research and may not be precisely friendly for beginners as it is less instructional and more about executing the moves. Also, you will not find much use of it for assets that are not in the U.S. or U.S. centric.

Charles Schwab. This platform is excellent for new traders as it gives you the education and support that you will need. It has low fees while offering you $0.65 per contract, all depending on the number of trades that you will make.

However, through its IdeaHub, you will get trade ideas that you can execute through its StreetSmart platforms.

However, this broker does not offer you better customization, which means you will need to use it on default for a better interface. Also, the margin rates tend to be a little higher than what other brokers will offer you.

Trading in options will be an excellent way for you to begin to generate passive income without giving or spending too much. However, as we have seen throughout the chapter, your analysis will need to guide you. Before getting into options trading, you will need to take your time to understand your market and learn how to make both fundamental and technical analysis.

Through making the right choices, you will learn how you can make your position and time your entry into the market. Once you complete it, then you identify the strategies that you will use to increase your chances of making gains when you trade.

One positive about options trading over stock trading is that, when you pay the premium, you mitigate yourself from losses. This low cost means that you will then have the potential for limitless profits. Yet, as we have said, swing trading remains a high-risk venture. You will still have the risk hanging above your head even when you pay your premiums. However, you put yourself in a better position with options trading.

So, to recap the fundamentals of how to swing trade on options:

Strategies: Swing trading on options is very different from swing trading on stocks. As such, you will need a better breakdown of the procedure that you will use correctly for swing trading on options. So, understand the strategies; long put, long call, protective collar, and protective put, among others. You will trade easier when you do.

Procedure: Once you know your strategy, then it comes down to process. You will need to understand how you will analyze your market and then follow through the right steps.

Brokers: They will make or break your trading motives. When you find the right one who knows and understands the assets, you will gain an advantage. We have mentioned a few that will help you work through the options trading, along with how they will work for you as a beginner and their pros and cons.

Chapter 5: Financial Instruments, Tools, and Platforms

Financial Instruments

Financial markets have hundreds of thousands and, in some cases, millions of people brought together from around the globe to trade a wide range of financial instruments. Taking into account that the financial market is the biggest, there are various instruments or securities that a trader can take advantage of to trade as well as to squeeze in some tangible profits.

Financial instruments are divided into five major categories which include equities, forex, indices, bonds, and commodities. Taking into account the wide range of financial instruments, there are several factors to consider before trading in any of the instruments named above.

What to Consider During the Selection of Financial Instruments

- **Volatility:** This refers to the capability of financial securities to upsurge and then fall completely or sharply. It can be compared to a two-sided sword that can turn out to be a curse and a blessing at the same time. High volatility tends to favor the traders who know how to maneuver the financial markets simply because it allows them to harvest profits many times. Nonetheless, the mishap that comes hand in hand with high volatility is that losses tend to accrue much faster.

- **Liquidity:** Liquidity refers to how easy it is to sell and buy a financial instrument at a particular time. Instruments that have high liquidity tend to be traded easily because a trader can enter and leave a position easily.
- **Low costs of the transaction:** A financial instrument whose transaction cost is significantly low is perfect because it allows a trader to get maximum profits on any particular trade. Different brokers have varying trading costs for various financial instruments.
- **Availability of information:** If a trader is looking forward reap maximum profit trading in a particular security or instrument, there is a need to have free-flowing information at his disposal every time. News alters the prices every time, and it is only reasonable for a trader to trade in a security whose information or news is readily accessible.

The Five Major Financial Instruments

Forex

To begin with, the foreign exchange market is the biggest market around the globe. This explains why it brings forth some of the most profitable financial instruments for traders to trade on a day-to-day basis. The forex market is accountable for over $4,000,000,000,000 in average volume every day.

Foreign exchange (forex) can be referred to as the process of buying and selling currencies by simply capitalizing on changes or fluctuations in the prices of currency pairs. Some of the foreign exchange instruments that are commonly used in trading involve currency pairs from the world's greatest economies including GBP/USD, EUR/USD, USD/CHF, USD/GPY, and many others.

Foreign exchange instruments are arguably the most appropriate to trade in because they are relatively stable. Taking into account that the forex instruments are usually available 24 hours a day, every week makes them completely ideal or appropriate to trade in at any particular time of the day irrespective of jurisdiction. Also, brokers in forex tend to provide sizeable leverage that simplifies or lightens the burden for traders to engage in trade that they would have not been able to afford in normal circumstances because of their capital.

Foreign exchange instruments are equally appropriate for day trading (short-term) because they tend to offer high levels of liquidity. They also bring with them high volatility that enables traders to easily take advantage of or capitalize on short-term fluctuations of prices.

Nonetheless, traders should create a habit of avoiding currency pairs that are exotic because they do not have the required levels of liquidity. Besides, brokers also have a habit of charging enormously on the spreads of this kind of currency pairs. In the long run, this makes it extremely difficult to generate maximum profits in the case of short-term price movements.

Stock Indices

Stock indices are responsible for highlighting how wider stock markets have performed as well as how a portion of the entire market has performed. This kind of indices usually indicates the stocks of particular companies from a particular sector. In other cases, this listing may be based on what their market cap is. Usually, the prices of given stocks are weighted as a means of making it easier for investors to carry out a comparison of the profits that a given investment has raked in.

Stock indices could be used as representations of how a particular country has performed economically as well as a representation of the stock market all over the world. In the stock indices section, S & P 500 is ranked among the top-notch financial instruments.

The S & P 500 can be termed as a diverse financial instrument because it takes in stocks that belong to 500 companies or even more. That being said, if the indices perform significantly well, this is a reflection of a good movement in the entire stock market of the United States.

Equities

To add on to stock indices, equities represent other extraordinary financial instruments. Rather than gaining more and more exposure through stock indices, somebody can decide to buy and sell individual stocks of given companies. Stock trading gives a trader the ability to enjoy owning a company or organization depending on how many shares he/she decides to buy.

Stock is part one of the most preferred financial instruments simply because they bring along relatively high liquidity. Volatility, as well as trading volumes, tends to vary on a day-to-day basis, and this gives traders the chance to capitalize on any subtle price fluctuations or movements.

Stocks from some of the top-ranking companies are the most preferred in the case of day trading considering the high degrees of volatility and liquidity that they come with. This kind of stock can include Microsoft, Apple, Google, and Amazon Qualcomm Intel, among many others.

Whenever you trade inequities, you need to observe and notice some of the things that affect the prices of stocks in one way or another. To begin with, at the very top of this list are earnings that come forth after three months. These earnings can alter the prices of shares simply because they act as indicators of how a good or bad company is doing financially as well as the company's long-term prospects. The price of a stock could upsurge on investors and by taking a look at data and reducing it to show that the value of the company will rise as time goes by.

How analysts rate stocks every day also affects the prices of shares in one way or another. Analysts usually carry out detailed analysis and inspection of companies, and in the long run, they give the traders recommendations or suggestions on how they should go about the business of buying and selling. Most of the time, this kind of report usually triggers price movements.

Also, news from the industry sector can have a dominant effect, hence affecting how individual stock will be priced in the long run. Therefore, an analysis of industry news must be carried out regularly whenever you opt to trade equities.

Commodities

Commodities that are in liquid forms such as silver, crude oil, and gold equally provide an avenue for traders to trade on the financial markets. Commodities being a form of financial instruments give traders an option to diversify and venture beyond stock indices and equities.

A trader can sell and buy a wide range of commodities through future agreements on exchanges. This kind of financial instruments is divided into five major categories that include, meat and livestock commodities, agricultural commodities, precious metals, energy, as well as industrial metals.

In the metal section, the financial instrument traded mostly includes silver, copper, gold, and platinum. In the energy category, crude oil is the undisputed leader after which gasoline and natural gas come in next. The meat and livestock section attracts a great part of its demand on pork bellies, lean hogs, as well as live cattle feeders. Under the agricultural category, the most traded financial instruments are soybeans, cocoa, rice, corn, and coffee.

In commodities, prices are driven by demand and forces of supply. Therefore, in the case that there is a limited supply on a particular commodity, the result most of the time would be that the prices will go up, essentially on high demand. Gold can be categorized as the undisputed financial instrument in the commodity category because traders perceive it as dependable and reliable as a means of protecting value.

Traders who are more experienced also resort to precious metals as a way of shielding themselves from the tough times that come by because of inflation or during periods where currencies undergo devaluation. Crude oil is also another commodity that is mostly used as a financial instrument because changes in the outputs of oil wells from all over the globe significantly alter prices, thus giving traders a chance to capitalize or take advantage of the swing in prices.

Grains, as well as other agricultural products, tend to be completely volatile and ideal for trading especially during summer. A limited supply of agricultural products and an increase in a population provides trading activities most of the time because they result in price movements.

Government Treasuries and Exchange-Traded Funds

To sum up, the major financial instruments discussed above are government treasuries, which is also referred to as bonds, and exchange-traded funds (ETFs). Exchange-traded funds refer to investment funds that are tasked with tracking how particular commodities, bonds, or sector indices perform.

Exchange-traded funds are tasked with covering a variety of assets that range from bonds, currencies, stocks, as well as commodities and real estate. Whenever a trader purchases an exchange-traded fund, he/she is purchasing funds to a list that is trying to copy or reproduce the performance of a particular fundamental asset.

Rather than trading indices or equities, a section of traders opts to buy exchange-traded funds because they make trades just like stocks. ETFs can be purchased and sold on a margin because their prices change all through a trading period. They also equally provide better diversification and mitigate risks because they are only tasked with tracking how fundamental indices perform.

On the other hand, government treasuries make up some of the most recommended financial instruments because of the safety net that they bring along whenever it narrows down to being exposed to risk. There is virtually no other financial instrument that comes with assurance whenever it comes to profits as treasuries/bonds do. This is the main reason why they could overcome tough vicious waves in the financial markets as some of the most ideal tool for investment by investors who are focused on raking in enormous amounts of profits.

Treasury instruments are subdivided into T-bills that take the most limited time to mature, probably between 4-52 weeks. For instance, T-notes are referred to as the mid-range government treasuries because they take a minimum of about two years and a maximum of about ten years to mature. On the other hand, T-bonds are suitable for investors who are seeking long-term investments because they might take up to 30 years to mature.

Financial Instrument to Trade-In

The most appropriate financial instrument to trade depends on various factors. To begin with, the amount of capital that somebody has will greatly determine the instrument they can trade. For example, choosing to invest in government treasuries will always require the trader to have a specific amount of capital in comparison to the foreign exchange markets where there is always leverage on offer.

The foreign exchange market is proving itself to be the ideal destination for individuals seeking to begin their careers as investors in the financial markets. Why? This is because the forex market brags about an income of about four trillion dollars every day. A statistic that ranks it as the market with the highest liquidity thus making it appropriate for entering and exiting trades easily to capitalize on small price fluctuations.

Another reason why most people trade forex instruments is that it requires low capital in comparison to other instruments. A trader who is just beginning needs between $100 to $1,000 to open an account and proceeds to trade in a wide range of forex securities.

Bottom line: The financial markets will toss a wide range of financial instruments at your feet. Nonetheless, that does not insinuate that all the instruments discussed above will be helpful or effective for you. Having a clear comprehension of particular security as well as the issues that can alter its price is the best way to come up with an investment venture that will be profitable in the long run.

An investor should never settle on financial security until they get enough knowledge on the factors that can affect its normal operations. Settling on a financial instrument simply because most investors trade is a recipe for failure.

Best Stock Trading Platforms for Buying Stocks

Swing Trading with TD Ameritrade

TD Ameritrade refers to a brokerage platform that is publicly traded, and it is tasked with offering investment products to investors all over the globe. Having been ranked as the best brokerage firm, TD Ameritrade is an undisputed leader in the swing trading industry. It offers swing traders several options to carry outswing trades. These include a desktop-based platform, a mobile phone application, as well as a web-based avenue.

The web-based avenue or platform is undoubtedly an ideal option for successful swing trading because it conducts or carries out trades exceptionally, but it does not contain any advanced analytics or tools that are available on the desktop. The desktop's Thinkorswim has the most efficient analytics and tools that are crucial for swing traders who are fully immersed in the business. Also, the mobile trading application that is ranked as the best trading platform on the Apple Play Store is an efficient option for traders who are always moving up and down but do not want to miss out on fast-changing trends in the market. All three platforms discussed above can be used freely outside the normal trading costs.

Pros of TD Ameritrade: TD Ameritrade is the current industry leader that offers a wide range of options that not every brokerage firm can offer to swing traders. TD Ameritrade offers a commission to new clients plus a bonus of up to $600. If a trader is not ready to jump into their swing trading plan instantly, they offer him a different option—paper trading. This is a test account that allows a trader to test a trading plan without necessarily committing actual money. As soon as the trader feels like he/she is ready to dive into real trading, the benefits only multiply. The average speed of execution of TD Ameritrade places at under 1/10 of a second.

Thinkorswim is inarguably one of the most efficient platforms that TD Ameritrade has to do offer and the most preferred platform by many swing traders unless the trader is only left with the mobile phone application option. Considering that swing traders depend entirely on technical analysis to take note of trends and consequently take advantage of those trends of those to reap profits, the tools availed in the desktop platform are not valuable. The reliability and speed of Thinkorsiwm enable traders to do away with losses as fast as possible if they have any chances of capitalizing returns before the market swings.

Ally Invest

Ally Invest has been consistently ranked among some of the best online platforms for swing trading. Ally Invest as a brokerage firm offers traders some of the most subsidized stock prices as well as buying and selling prices in the swing trading industry for about $4 for every trade along with the volume discounts. Ally Invest also offers options trading which is equally affordable because it costs about half a dollar for every option contract.

This platform also streams charts, markets snapshots, historical information, and quotes online, as well as across all devices with the help of its mobile phone application.

Ally invest equally offers managed funds, retirement accounts, as well as online bank services, in case a trader wants to consolidate his investments, do a check as well as save in one place. Their customer service is also top-notch, where there is an able support team all around the clock.

E-Trade

This is not just a swing trading platform but is also ranked among some of the best brokerage firms for several reasons such as its ability to have instant access to data, analysis, as well as research in its brokerage avenue.

After all, it is common knowledge that in Swing trading, nothing is as valuable as real-time and historical data that gives the trader the power to act on all the best stocks available. E-Trade also equally offers a wide range of knowledge-based resources such as blog posts, webinars, and news.

It is not the cheapest brokerage firm, but its commissions are not very steep. It sells its stocks at a price of about $7, inclusive of volume discount, whereas the prices of options begin at half a dollar for every contract.

Best Stock Trading Tools for Backtesting and Technical Analysis

Successful swing trading requires seamless, intuitive and platforms. Stock trading platforms refer to several computer programs that make it possible for traders to trade in financial securities like currencies and stocks in this scenario, and they also play a crucial role in helping traders improve how they carry out their stock-picking through technical and fundamental analysis features. Some software also can support transactions. Brokers offer this software either at a discounted price or for free. In some cases, this software is offered as incentives to bring about a certain amount or degree of the trade.

What to look for in trading software?

Real-time and historical data. Real-time data refers to information that is provided instantly or after a shorty while from the time information was disseminated. In as much as numerous websites promise that they will provide you with real-time information, they might delay for periods of up to twenty minutes. Real-time information is vital for the trader because even a subtle swing or change in the price of an instrument may result in significant returns or even losses. On the other, handicap data or information is equally important because the prices of financial instruments move in noticeable trends and patterns which tend to recur over time.

Analytical methods and strategies. Normally, swing traders use several rules based on technical or fundamental analysis. In some cases, both fundamental and technical analysis may be used. Therefore, trading software gives traders the ability to manage and control open positions. In some cases, the types of orders might include market order that refers to purchasing and selling at the current price and pending order, which means that transactions go through a price that was predetermined.

Live and breaking news. The financial market is capricious and it tends to move depending on many developments such as corporate and geopolitical news as well as economics. Considering that stocks have high volatility, it requires that if traders intend to reap commendable returns, they have to have a quick reaction to the news that moves the market through a source of news that should always be up to date.

Stock screener. This refers to a tool used by swing traders to do filtration of stocks based on particular criteria.

Backtesting software. This software allows a swing trader to test a particular trading plan using old or historical information, this serves as a means of verifying how effective a given plan is. It involves putting a certain strategy into action for a given period after which analysis is done on the results based on the profit and risk perspective.

Below are the tools used in swing trading.

Tickeron

Whenever it comes to comprehending trends or patterns in the stock market, there is a wide range of variables that come on board. Tickeron makes this process simpler with its artificial intelligence software that can carry out trend analysis as well as making predictions in trends. It supports its artificial intelligence predictions with or historical information as well as elevated levels of confidence in making predictions to ensure that the results are top-notch.

Tickerson's ability to predict trends leverages machine learning and algorithms to spot and consequently alert you with patterns that will increase your chances of reaping maximum profits in the stocks you choose to trade. As soon as you subscribe to it, it offers the following products: alerts, trend analysis, progress on various instruments like currencies, forex, ETFs, and also cryptocurrency. Trend predictions give the traders tip-offs if a financial instrument is to be bearish, sideways, or bullish within a certain time.

Generally, trend predictions are a useful tool for swing traders because it equips the trader with numerous actionable plans of action

MarketSmith

Have you always been hunting for a better way to carry out your swing trade research? Do you feel like all you ever do is check and cross-check internet sites for information about the market? MarketSmith takes care of all these issues for you.

MarketSmith is undoubtedly one of the most comprehensive research avenues around. With MarketSmith, you can narrow everything down to one window irrespective of whether it is a stock chart, recognition of patterns, and a well-detailed list of ready to use promising stocks. MarketSmith can boost your confidence, optimize the time you dedicate to research, and set price alerts.

Tradingview

This software takes the biggest chunk in this category. This stock charting package boats of over a hundred in-built technical signals for carrying out analysis. The market caters to virtually all trading indicators and concepts and offers over five thousand custom-built indicators.

Tradingview's programming language enables a trader to come up with and share signals and custom studies because it can modify any study code and consequently create virtually any custom predictor from scratch.

In addition to essential information on companies, it equally gives you economic information, both globally and domestically, and also enables you to compare economic information.

From a social point of view, it has also put in place chat apps, chat forums, and a channel for sharing what your analysis is with other people with just one click. This platform also allows you to stay in contact with many other traders all around the world.

Yewno Edge

This is the perfect solution to data overload for individual investors and also financial professionals. This platform aggregates alternative and fundamental data to provide traders with insights that they can work on. This insinuates that it cuts down the amount of time spent reading through large amounts of news articles and data and instead spend more time trading.

This platform enables traders to evaluate how a company is exposed to concepts that are ill-defined and abstract such as data privacy. It can also come up with portfolio plans around this kind of concept. Traders are also permitted to leverage it in such a way that shows data beyond what a company chooses to show.

StockCharts

Investing in swing trade can be frustrating at times, but with the help of tools such us as StockCharts, trading can be made a lot easier. StockCharts enable you to see the market from a different point of view in a way that will help you improve how you manage your portfolio as well as finding promising trading activities faster.

Trusted by hundreds of thousands of investors all-round the world, StockCharts assist investors in coming up with the web's best financial charts as fast as possible. With StockCharts, you can create larger, bigger, and more sophisticated charts that make the process of trading much easier. You can also carry out custom scans to look for new investments and trades as well as setting automatic tip-offs that. The availability of daily market analysis from the industry's most experienced technicians enables you to follow these technicians and take a look at the most recent charts that they are watching.

With StockCharts, you can carry out active charting wherever you go. In swing trading, you have to be aware that the markets do not care about anybody irrespective of the importance of what you are doing. That is why you require a real-time tool for charting that you can use wherever you go, anytime and on any virtually every device.

Considering that StockCharts have been designed specifically for the modern-day trader, it puts the industry's most valuable resources and tools in the palms of your hands with no need to install any software or stressing cases of compatibility. Regardless of whether you are using a laptop, smartphone, or desktop, you can easily get access to all that you need from a web-enabled device.

StockCharts also has a well-stocked toolkit for your entire trading process. Irrespective of whether you are a regular investor or you are looking after your retirement accounts, StockCharts provide you with everything you require to strategize, organize, and implement virtually any trading system as follows:

- It helps you take note of the opportunities that are most promising with the help of your advanced surveillance tools.
- It helps you pinpoint the most appropriate point of entry. Thereafter, you can follow up on the open position that you are in and tracking your portfolio with the help of the chart.
- Finally, when it gets to a point where you have to sell, StockCharts will assist you in coming up with a perfect exit point.

Just like anything else, at the end of the day, the choice that an investor makes narrows down to his/her needs. Therefore, as an investor, from the software tools discussed above, whether, it is a tool or platform, pinpoint what you think is important or what you think will work perfectly for you and implement it appropriately.

Chapter 6: Within the Technical Analysis Focus on Charting Basics, Indicator Tools and Patterns

As outlined earlier, swing trading refers to a style of trading that attempts to capture gain in a stock over a specified period. It is worth noting that swing traders use technical analysis to look for trading opportunities. Technical analysis refers to a trading discipline that is employed to evaluate investments as well as trading opportunities through the art of analyzing some statistical trends that are in most cases gathered from any trading activity. In other words, various aspects are involved in any investment plan. Unlike a fundamental analysis that attempts in evaluating the security scrutiny intrinsic value, the technical report focuses on some of the patterns of the movement of price, signals of trading, and various analytical charting tools to evaluate the strength as well as weakness of the security.

In trading, technical analysis can be utilized on any security with the historical trading center. The aspects include stocks, commodities, currencies, other securities as well as fixed income. In an attempt to comprehend this type of analysis, a lot of scholars have used stock to explore the art of technical analysis. However, this form of the technical report can be utilized in any security. In other words, technical analysis is more prevalent in commodities and forex markets where trades focus on short-term price movements.

The Basics of Technical Analysis

As stock analysts, or people who understand that technology, was first introduced by Charles Dow in his theory published in the late 1800s. There were several analysts and scholars such as William, Robert, as well as Edson and Magee who contributed to the development of the theory. In the modern-day, the art of technical analysis has significantly evolved to include hundreds of signals and patterns. The event has occurred gradually after inductive research carried out in the years. One of the critical aspects of technical analysis is that analysts believe that the past trading activities and the price changes of any form of security might be valuable indicators of the performance of price movements in the market. The aspect indicates that they may use the independent technical analysis of other research efforts or preferably in combination with different concepts of the intrinsic value considerations as well as the most often convictions that are based in statically charts of security as shown below. The Market Technicians Association (MTA) is one most popular groups that supports the art of technical analysts in their investments.

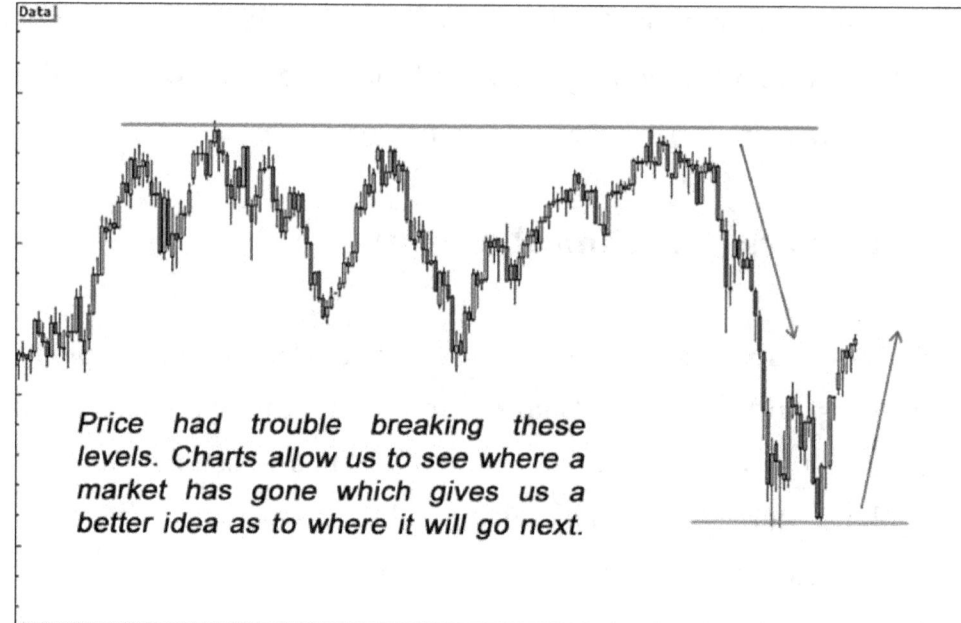

Price had trouble breaking these levels. Charts allow us to see where a market has gone which gives us a better idea as to where it will go next.

Assumptions in Technical Analysis

Two methods are utilized in the art of analyzing securities and making an investment decision. The art of deciding at times tend to be technical since bad decision-making leads to wrong results. Also, the art of analyzing securities is essential because it is a requirement that determines whether the protection of choice is working or not. In other words, the art of making decisions and deciding the kind of investment to take depends on the analysis that is done of the stock at hand. The report plays a critical role in outlining some of the future aspects that are vital. Analysts use past data and the performance of previous data in describing and identifying the future performance of the stock in question. The prospects are crucial in that they help in the art of making decisions as the investor uses these prospects and results of the analysis to estimate the earning they expect from a particular form of investment.

The methods that are utilized in the analysis include fundamental and technical analysis. Fundamental analysis involves the art of analyzing a company's financial statement in the art of determining its value in the business. In that fundamental analysis, the balance sheet, and another financial statement is utilized to estimate the value of the premises. The aspect is critical in the sense that it helps in determining the price of the shares. The analysts use fundamental to check on the history of the premises. In other words, one uses the financial statement to check how the premises have been doing in an attempt of increasing its capital base. The art of profit-making, as well as suffering loss, determines the future value of the organization. Such aspects are essential in helping investors make decisions about whether they will invest with specific organizations. The element is linked to the fact that all investors enter business intending to make profits. Thus, they will choose to spend with the organization that has better prospects and one that has been stable for a couple of years. Organizations make loses, but how they deal with loses and the stability of the premises determines how stable it is as well as the risks involved. However, assumptions that rarely make profits and keep avoiding taking risks indicate that they are relatively unstable. Investors realize the risks involved in choosing such firms as a means of investment. The fundamental analysis is more into the statistical analysis of the price movements.

The technical analysis is more detailed because it attempts in understanding the market sentiments that are behind the price trends through the art of looking for patterns and trends instead of checking on the fundamental attributes of security. According to Charles Dow, markets are efficient with specific values that influence the securities, but market price movements are not only pure but random. Thus, they bare more identifiable trends and patterns that tend to repeat themselves. In other words, investors or analysts utilize such aspects to determine whether organizations or premises are doing well instead of making a continuous loss.

There is an efficient market hypothesis that essentially means that the price of a security at any point may reflect the information of the organization. In other words, the market price of a security at any given time accurately reflects the information or rather the real value of the guard. The aspect indicates that some assumptions are made concerning the marked price, which is made with the mindset that the market price reflects the total sum of knowledge of the market participants. In other words, the market price is determined by several individuals, and that the pricing considers several relevant factors. The assumptions made might be correct and might be affected by the fact that the security might be having some shortcomings. In other words, if there are shortcomings on the safety, there are chances that the price or rather its competitive nature in the market will significantly reduce. However, technical analysis works if the market is weakly efficient. The aspect allows direct scrutiny of all the elements that are involved hence the long-term influence.

The other assumption states that price changes are not random, in that organizations may not think of changing the price of their stocks or rather their shares within a twinkle of an eye. The aspect is linked to the fact that before a change in pricing is done, numerous elements ought to be considered. In other words, all the stakeholders, as well as the marketers, let alone the suppliers, ought to be considered before any decision is made. Thus, the technical analysts can check the market trends both on a short-term and long-term basis as it allows the trend analysis, wherein the analysts can identify the stable prices and trends that operate within a particular organization. They help in identifying stable organizations and these making profits with an increasing trend. The art of understanding these trends and patterns is essential in making decisions. Investors look for relatively stable organizations and these can withstand the challenges in the market, so they will prefer venturing in trading with promising premises. These trends try to scrutinize some of the factors that have been enabling an organization to make profits or keep suffering loses. There are factors or an aspect that affects an organization for it to keep making profits or suffer from loses. The trend is essential in that organization, or relatively stable premises, tend to attract more investors as compared to those with fewer capitalization aspects or weak in terms of maintaining supper trends. However, a trailing stop is a trade order, and it means that the stop-loss price is not fixed to a single dollar amount but is set at a particular percentage or amount that is below the current market price.

In the modern market, the technical analysis considers three main assumptions that are essential in helping investors make decisions. Assumptions tend to explore the entire market and provide detailed information about the premises in question, which include:

Market discounts everything. There are a lot of experts in marketing analysis that tend to criticize technical analysis. Technical analysis only considers the price movements and tends to ignore other fundamental factors that are critical in shaping the art of marketing. The technical report examines the trends of the pricing of shares—yes, other aspects are involved for the shares to be sold at that price. However, one of the elements assumed by a technical analyst is that everything from the premises to the broad market psychology is already priced in the stock. The aspect allows the technical analysts to ignore other factors that are involved in making decisions. In other words, technical analysts assume that all the other factors that ought to be considered while making decisions on prices of shares were put into consideration. Thus, they only focus on the remaining art of analyzing the price movements, and they view the products in the form of supply and demand for a particular stock in the market rather than individual factors affecting the pricing of shares from a specific organization.

Price movement trends. Technical analysts tend to believe that different trends affect the pricing of shares. There is a belief that price moves in three shifts: short-term, medium-term, and long-term trends. The analysts move with the confidence that the stock price may continue the particular pasta trend that is more erratic. In most cases, technical trading strategies are based on such an assumption. In other words, some trends affect the pricing of shares in the market as shown below.

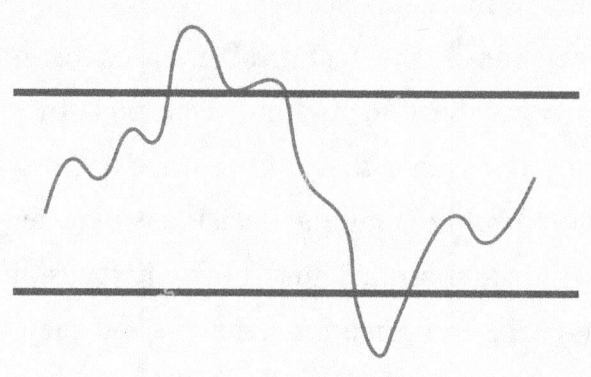

In most cases, the changes tend to affect the organization; hence, the investors. Those organizations that are about to maintain their prices at a specific rate indicates that they are relatively stable, so they are likely to keep pricing making profits. Investors will prefer risking their funds on such premises as there are hopes of getting more funds or instead of making more profits in the long-run. On the other hand, assumptions that cannot maintain their prices tend to be less stable and attract fewer investors, so they are likely to make that reflects in the pricing of shares.

History repeats itself. Technical analysts tend to believe that no matter the time is taken or the pricing of shares history tends to repeat itself. There is some marketing psychology that tends to bring some aspects of predictability based on emotions such as fear or rather an excitement. There are also certain emotions or character that brings some elements of repetition in terms of price movements. In most cases, the technical analyst uses chart patterns to try and analyze feelings as well as the subsequent actions for them to understand the trend. There is no need for involving a lot of factors that tend to affect the pricing of shares to study on the movements. However, the art of considering the history or rather the trends in a few seasons tend to offer help that enables analysts to make relatively accurate predictions. Even the analysis used for more than 100 years ago can be utilized to estimate or make predictions based on the season at hand. The aspect is linked to the fact that certain elements tend to relate to the emotions or the aspects that were affecting the pricing of shares or stick then. Thus, based on the feelings perceived in a particular season, the analysts can identify or instead predict the price of these shares shortly. The art of understanding the trends or rater the number of shares is critical in the sense that it allows investors to make the right decisions as they choose the firm to invest in. Some premises show some aspects of stability even with continuous market changes.

Utilization of Technical Analysis

As outlined earlier, technical analysis attempts to forecast on the art of price movements of virtually any item or tradable instrument. Thus, any questions that are subject to demand and supply can be subjected to technical analysis. Such issues or rather devices include bonds, stock, futures as well as currency pairs. When the demand for these products in cases, the price tends to rise as the supply tends to increase. On the other hand, if the amount is relatively high, the demand tends to reduce, and the owners or rather, the suppliers tend to reduce their prices to attract more investors.

In the same way, the technical analysis considers such changes and identifies the trends that are followed by each organization to come up with charts or rather patterns that are critical in explaining what lies in the future. Some people regard technical analysis as the study of demand and supply forces that are reflected in the market price movements of a security. In other words, technical analysis tends to track the price changes and breakdowns the track numbers other than the price of the share. It allows the analysts to view the patterns of these changes and make predictions. Investors need such predictions before they can make decisions as it opens the mind and makes the right decisions. They can select organizations with better predictions, hence making supernormal profits in the future as well.

As an investor, you need to consider the risks involved in any trend before investing. In some cases, you may need something, and you are not sure where to get it. You may be torn in between two things, and you are not sure which the best is. In such a case, you need a broker to help you out. A broker is a middleman who will be in charge of bringing together a buyer and the seller. You will mostly find the brokers in the business world, and they broke aiming to get some commission. A broker can either be a person or a company, and they will arrange transactions on your behalf. They can either be insurance, a commodity as well as stockbrokers.

A broker will be responsible for bringing forth a seller or a buyer and will transact on their behalf, but there are no cases where they can represent them at the same time. They will either provide you with information as well as advice about a particular trade. They will do that at a cost, and that is where they mostly get their income from. That means they have a lot of information and will invest a lot so that they can know more about the trade they are in.

A broker will aim at establishing a relationship with a lot of people that seem to be prospective clients. They will do all in their reach so that they can have the best connections with both the sellers and the buyers in trade and conducts the best deals ever. Research is part of what they do from time to time so that they can have full information at their disposal. Brokers will analyze raw data to establish whether a particular investment is an excellent risk. They will do all they can to provide resources that will help you to manage risk.

There are hundreds of signals and patterns that have been developed by various scholars to support the art of technical analysis. Technical analysts have been developing numerous trading systems that are helpful in forecasting and predicting trade movements. Multiple indicators are majorly focused on identifying the marketing trend so that they can offer or outline the areas that need to be focused on. The analysts thus determine the strength of a direction so as they can predict whether the pattern will change or persist. In most cases, technical indicators and charting patterns, are vital in offering such predictions. Such models and symbols include trend lines, moving averages, momentum indicators, as well as moving averages. In general, technical analysis focuses on price trends, chart patterns, volume and momentum indicators, oscillators, moving averages, and support and resistance levels.

Patterns and Indicators

In technical analysis, the transition that is perceived in the process of falling and rising trends is observed as price patterns. Thus, technical analysts understand price patterns as a recognizable configuration of the movements in price that is identified by the art of utilizing a series of trend lines or preferably curves. When a price pattern signals a change in the direction of a trend, it is perceived as a reversal pattern. In most cases, a continuous mode occurs when the trend tends to continue in the same direction without the art of being altered or changing in any form. Investors, in most cases, prefer patterns that are relatively stable and keep moving in the right direction. A trend line that is angled in the right angle tends to experience higher prices as compared to the declining one. There are times where current movements tend to have a brief pause, but a continuation is perceived when the trend continues existing. The technical analysts thus use such analysis to identify patterns and trends that ought to be followed by investors and make profits. Technical analysts are equipped with knowledge that can be utilized in understanding the marketing trends. Such analysis is critical in offering a forecast based on history and a true reflection of the performance of the firm. Most stable firms tend to have trends that are ever-increasing hence higher chances of making profits.

Trend Lines in Technical Analysis

A pattern is well identified using a series of lines as well as curves that help explore what terms as trend lines are. The trend lines are utilized by technical analysts to sport areas or resistance as well as support in a chart area. Trend lines are the straight lines that are drawn on a chart to connect a series of peaks as well as troughs. They are angled up occur where the prices are experiencing mountains.

In most cases, the ups are connected with the lows as a means of indicating how the price has been rising. A downtrend line, on the other hand, occurs when the prices are experiencing lower highs and lower lows. The peaks are relatively small and the troughs trend in the very lows. In such seasons, the investors or rather the owners of premises tend to make loses, especially if they had an investor in high seasons or somewhat when the trend lines were angled in the up angle.

Trend Lines Basics

The art of understanding the direction of any underlying trend is one of the essential aspects that are utilized by analysts to offer the necessary predictions. The policy used by these analysts is that of probability and enhances the art of being successful trade as it ensures that the market forces work in favor of the investor. Downward-sloping trends indicate that there is an excess supply of securities. The aspect shows that there are fewer buyers hence the art of lowering the prices. In such moments, investors are usually encouraged to avoid holding the shares for long. There are situations where the downgrading continues up to a point where one makes loses in a low. Thus, investors tend to release their shares and avoid further drops. However, there are cases where the upwards trends tend to increase and shows no signs of reducing. In such situations, investors are at times advised to hold the shares a little bit as they wait for the prices to increase.

However, it reaches a point where these profits or rather the prices don't grow anymore, so investors are encouraged to release their shares and make profits as shown below.

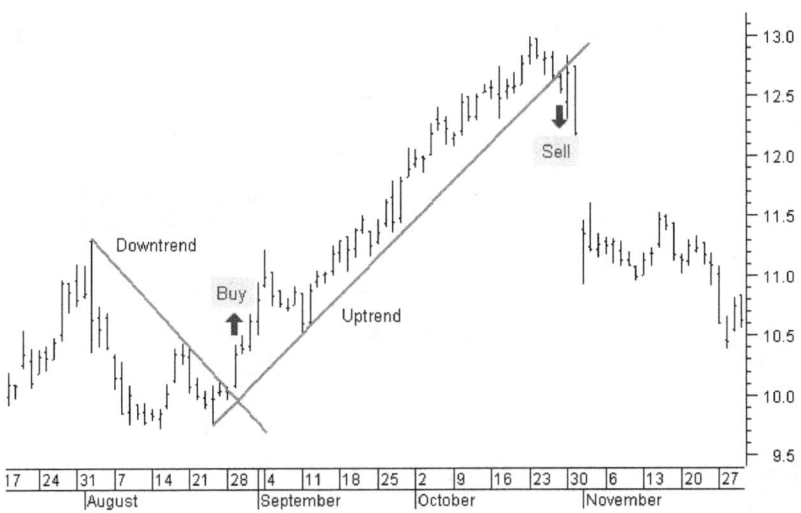

On the other hand, when the prices are low, some investors join the market and wait for the trend lines to reach their peak before releasing their shares. The art of understanding these trends is what makes investors remain in the premises or preferably in the market following the art of making profits seasons after seasons. However, there are cases where these trends fail to augur well, and the opposite of the expectations happens. In such situations, investors are forced to suffer as they wait for prices to hike.

Trend lines tend to differ depending on the market, time frame, and slope on the route involved. Some trends tend to show a downward or slightly upward aspect for months or even days. However, there are some which tales a couple of minutes to change. Others become bold and tend to remain constant. Such aspects are critical in the sense that they help in making decisions as well as projections at hand. Investors prefer to risk their funds in relatively stable organizations or those that keep making profits. The aspect guarantees success as well as an increased point of making profits.

Support and Resistance

Trend lines are relatively tools that are utilized in gauging the performance or rather the direction of a given asset. Also, they can be used by traders to predict the resistance and support, which means that the trend lines are used in identifying the levels on a chart beyond which the price of a particular item. It helps in the identification of areas of entries in the business. The support refers to a price level where the downtrend can be expected to pause due to the concentration of demand. So when the price of shares drops, the need for shares tends to increase hence forming a support line as shown below.

On the other hand, the resistance zones tend to arise when the sell-off prices grow. Once the areas of resistance and support are identified, it provides valuable potential trade exit and entry points. In most cases, entry points are the points where the prices are relatively declining hence increased demand. Traders tend to exit the market when the prices are relatively high. In most cases, if you are a trader, you will look for opportunities to enter the market. It is a great way to help you to identify the opportunities that are there in the swing trade. It is the most popular strategy that will help you to indicate the direction a particular trend is taking. Whether it is a reversal of an upward movement and has two averages that move from time to time, when the two standards cross, they will lead to the generation of the buying as well as selling signals. The two lines are as well likely to cross above the signal line you have the opportunity to get into the trade. That will enable you to buy any item that you need. Wait for the two paths to cross, and they will create a signal for a business in the opposite direction. You need to be quick before the swing traders withdraw from the trade. These strategies can be put into use and will help you to know the trading opportunities that are there in any market that you have an interest in. Use the best approach to apply these strategies, and you will benefit significantly from them. Seek to find out more about swing trade and the technical indicators and the signals that they show.

You will be in a position to predict the price pattern both in the present time as well as in the future. There are brokers out there in the market who will do all they can afford so that investors will not suffer much loss. Stop-loss-order is a strategy that is widely known and will always protect you from suffering huge losses. If the price goes down to a certain level, the share will be sold regardless of the current price in the market to make sure that there will be no other losses. For stop-loss to be effective, it needs to be paired with a trailing stop. A trailing stop is a trade order, and it means that the stop-loss price is not fixed to a single dollar amount but is set at a particular percentage or amount that is below the current market price. When the prices shoot, the trailing stop as well goes up. In situations where the price is not rising any longer, the stop-loss will remain in the same place. That will be a way to shield an investor from suffering losses, and there will be profits realized since the price will get to higher levels.

Chapter 7: Guiding Principles, Rules, and Strategies of Swing Trading

Whatever level of trading you practice, you ought to know that your expectations for you to have a clear trading plan. In this case, swing trading is a market that takes several days to weeks, which focuses on amercing profits from stocks or other financial securities. Its goal is mainly to establish the price pattern of the trade and knowing the points to stake your odds. Remember that if you want to graduate from an amateur to a professional seller or buyer, then you have to adopt strategies in this exercise.

These strategies are very crucial as they make you follow a specific road map–if you are a navigator or an adventurer, you know what this means–because you follow paths, direction, and routes to lead you to where you want. You still make tracks and marks, and in case you get lost, you will always have a way of reclaiming your footsteps. That is the same thing with this kind of business. Swing trading is like a journey you need to follow for days. You ought to follow. You need to analyze the pattern to work with, which is the direction of where you are going. Just like the tracks, there must be the stop losses and the indicators to alarm you if you are heading to downfall.

Strategies and Rules of Swing Trading

Put your interest first in this trading. You have to know why you are trading and what you are looking for in that market. This area is susceptible because you are committing your resources. If you are not serious in this market, then it is not your playground. It is hurtful if you fail to achieve your target mark and to make substantial losses. If you are a newbie, you must have been taught on the technique to follow in reading the market. Therefore, you have to understand specific terms. You have to recognize the indicators and their significance, how to work with the brokerage account, and how to choose the best broker. The charts, technical analysis, and fundamental analysis are other essential information.

Note the overall direction of the trade. That is the pattern or the trend of the market. Use the telescopic view as much as you use the microscopic analysis. Microscopic analysis is the in-depth scanning of the market. Telescopic sight means that you are considering the trend on a large scale. Use both the fundamental and technical analysis to determine the direction. Follow the historical patterns of the market. What have been the past trends may influence even the future. Never focus on the short term trade only also if you are dealing with the swing trading. Yes, you may realize some benefits, but you are restricting yourself to the revenue which is found in the long run. In this case, the market direction is influenced by the news that affects the overall market. That is the fundamental analysis. News like the change of currency in a nation, merging of companies that impact the shares or other significant announcements affects the trading. Therefore, you have to be updated in this market news.

Be consistent in the route you take on the market. That is where one maintains the tactic to use in analyzing the market. Winners are not judged by the times they are successful but the energy they use to bounce back from a fall. They also have that identity of how they apply their methods; many are the times where even the experts fail to win. However, these people never give up, but they still use their failure as a stepping stone to achieving greatness. If you are too ambitious to get higher returns consistently, then you will be disappointed. In any way, if you maintain that approach in trading, you will finally find the breakthrough. Draw that market line in the position trading. Apply the same enter and the renter schemes you usually use. Do not be manipulated by the up-trending volatile market because once it hits the down-trending, you can blow up your account.

Trade intensely on the bullish patterns and go short in the weak direction. The receding point guarantees you risk, and the peak point is profitable. Use the indicator like the moving average and the relative price index. The moving average will help you to identify the direction of that price movement. The relative strength index helps one to know how the individual market is fairing with the market stock value. The point profitable in bearish is the relative strength index is trending downward. That is an alarm for you to sell before the value decreases. This is the same case as with the bullish sector. You must identify that area you buy a fruitful scheme before the price reduces. It is upon you to master the market carefully and identify these points accurately.

Trade to see the big picture of something. If you are that seller or buyer who trades for the short term profits, then it will be too bad for you. Perhaps, the short term is influenced by what will happen in the long run, and you may not know about it. Therefore, this can make you not fully understand the trend, which is costly to your business. Remember that even in the downtrend, there can be an upturn in the curve. That means the bearish line can twist and start to arise, so you are likely to make a mistake of selling at a loss if you are that marketer who does not think outside the box. Always look at the trend with different angles whenever you trade. You will realize that you will interpret something new or spot a favorable opportunity whenever you view the market with a different approach.

Appreciate the usage of multiple indicators in interpreting the pattern of the market. If you rely on one sign, you may fail to realize how the market is fairing. For example, if you fail to include the relative strength index indicator, how then would you compare your market with the market assets value? The price movement makes one use the moving average convergence/ divergence indicator. Talk of the candlesticks instrument and stochastic indicators; they are also significant measures of the trend. If they show the same results, then it is a good thing you are trading well. If you purchase with one tool, it may be wrong because the other may follow the opposite direction.

When entering or re-entering the trade aim trading at that starting point of a fruitful spot. You ought to recognize the position quickly to buy or sell your securities. It would be problematic to stake your odds at the endpoint because the momentum may have slowed down. That is comparing to that guy who spots a suitable spot and trades immediately. Thus, he or she will amerce sizeable returns before the trends decrease. At this point of good harvest, choose to buy the securities intensely. Buy low and sell high at this point because it is also a less risk zone. You will surely be in a better position to achieve maximally. Pay attention to the moving averages, which can decrease the momentum the market has picked. That is when these indicators show the goods overbought or oversold, which are sometimes susceptible to reversal.

Yes, you are dealing with swing trading, which only focuses on the short time frame. Do you know you can use a long-term chart like monthly ones to understand how the stocks are faring? You never know that until you are keen on interpreting the trends. Sometimes, you may find yourself failing to understand how the charts are working, but the extended run diagrams can enlighten you. Remember that these stocks are included in a variable timeframe. As much as you view the long-term frames, the short-term is necessary too. That is the microscopic view of them. These include the daily and hourly mark. That minimal issue like the hourly trend can influence the upcoming pattern even in weeks or months. This knowledge will help you to know whether to go to short or long trading. Remember that short marketing is preferred in the bearish scheme, while great marketing is suitable for an uptrend.

Establish a suitable stop-loss point and the trading zones. That depends on the features of the brokerage firm you are using. Open an account in a platform that has the stop losses and one can quickly draw the trading zones. A stop-loss is like an automatic detector that detects when you are about to make a loss. It will alarm on a specific point that would give you hefty loss. That is not forgetting about your selling or buying zones. It will automatically detect a profitable position that you can buy or sell. Understand how you usually trade, and the junctures which you believe are your stronghold. Note other areas that are risky where you have ever failed. In that juncture, you can set up the stop-loss as required

Carry out a SWOT analysis strategy to whether you are in a good position of trading. This system means that you know your strengths, weakness, opportunities, and threats. Consider your strongholds making transactions. These are the areas of expertise whenever you trade. They are also the skills in interpreting the indicator direction, the charts, the technical analysis, and using other tools to amerce returns. Even those professional traders you know still have the weakness. Perhaps their fault is failing to draw a stop loss, inability to readjust to an inflexible and volatile market. If the marketer fails to come up with a proper market plan that it is another liability. The potential opportunities are concerned with the informative news concerning the market. If a trader anticipates constructive communication that affects the market positively, then that is an opportunity at hand. If the indicators promise suitable results, it is still an opportunity. The treats may appear as the variable which influences the market negatively. For example, if you are trading currencies, then you hear that the interest rates are being lowered, and then it is a threat. Thus, before starting to trade, examine the market using the SWOT analysis program. You may not realize it, but it will assist you in making a positive stance.

Practice many times to obtain a rhythm of the trading. You may be that amateur without a plan; however, juggle with those figures and charts, and soon you will establish a tactic. When you subsequently fail, you will realize you are learning by your mistakes. The moment you make the trading scheme a hobby, you will attain much experience that will sharpen your skills. Try different approaches you know and realize which suits your interests. Consult also the specialists in this exercise who corrects you and directs you. Remember that even that expert was once an about what made them skilled is their reluctance and persistence. Therefore, by going with such a mindset, you will not fear to lose, and you will graduate to an expert.

Have a target value that you expect to harness at the end of the trading program. A convenient interchange scheme must guide that target. This scheme comprises the effective budgeting of accounts. That is where you have to be realistic in the amount to buy or sell. You cannot expect to harvest many fruits for the few plants you planted, so do not wait millions of dollars from the single penny you credited. That wining figures must be realistic and measurable with your account balance. If you operate with goals and targets, then is a strategy that keeps you focused? You can thus declare that at the end of the week, you need an absolute return and cut specific loses. Otherwise, you can target to have different and new strategies to work with every time.

These visions motivate you to work hard to accomplish them. They also encourage a person in skills training in the scheme.

Discover the best business plan for the exercise. Having no this scheme is like you are gambling with figures. It is thus a systematic and organized approach to conduct active trading. There are very many elements that make up this practice. One is the vision and the targets you want. Then, there is the budgeting of the money to use. You still need to design the excellent market orders which are profitable. That is based on the technical analysis and the fundamental analysis which determine them. Following the anticipated news and the price movements of the indicators, one thing you ought to know is that these elements affect the price movement. Another aspect to include is the re-entry and exit schemes in the plan. Moreover, add favorable policies that will be a routine for you to follow in the trading. You may identify the limit losses and the maximum earnings that one can use with the money you stake.

Be that flexible guy who can cap his or her account. That means you are separating your account into variable phases. It is not legible to work with one platform, and when bad luck strikes, it will be like hell when you lose your whole account balances. It is good to establish more than one account in which the trading scheme is different. That means you are dealing with diverse portfolios at a time. Remember that in swing trading, you may meet a volatile market which tempts you to stake all of your odds, and then all of a sudden 'oops, the money is lost.' Moreover, working in different accounts makes you diversify your earnings, that is to say, you can earn in one platform even if the other loses.

The professions know how to anticipate for the volatile market. Volatile markets are those sectors that have a sharp increase and decrease of the price movement. Their graph represents a very sloppy or steep curve. What would you do in such a scenario if you spotted a subtle curve? The first thing to do is to research why the market is behaving that way. Perhaps you were trading some stocks of a firm, and then you hear that the company has partnered with a dominant firm. What you expect in this case is that there will be many investors who will subscribe to those shares. Therefore the market cap goes in a bullish way. Then adopt the tactic of quickly buying when the volatility appears and selling at a profit before the upturn of the curve happens. Therefore in this scenario, you have to be updated on choosing the volatile stocks.

Whenever you make any returns, withdraw them as quickly as possible. Hey, not all of it because you still need to trade with an adequate amount. Take like half of it to prevent loss of all the profits you had made. Always have that target mark you want to withdraw into your account. You will realize that per day, you are making substantial fortunes, which you had already predicted. Otherwise, what would happen to that individual who had not withdrawn any amount at a bearish level? Then probably all the fortunes he or she made would indeed evaporate into thin air.

Why don't you draw the lines of the support and the resistance when swing trading. Those are technical analysis tools that help to prevent losses and ensure significant profit; it is also a risk management tool. On a bullish level or where buying is active, one should draw a suitable resistance line. This mark helps to identify the price zone on the chart below the market index where purchasing stock is strong enough. It also tends to limit any price movement going down the line, which would pressure a trader to sell. If there is falling on the price movement, the limit line will make it bounce back, so if you are planning to rebuy, consider that point which has significant momentum. There is a resistance level, which is the price movement above the market line that would prompt you to sell than to buy thereby causing the curve to proceed on a downtrend. In this case, the trader would seek to sell at the moment the market price would bounce off the resistance line. Another aspect to consider is how to position and locate the stop losses in both situations. For the resistance aspect, one would draw the stop loss above that line. The support level would prompt you to position your stop loss below that line.

Another strategy is channel trading. In this area, you would consider plotting the channel line. That is like a pathway or route that limits the buying or selling of securities in a particular area. Take an example of a downtrend where one would plot the channel mark. When the swing market bounces off the line of the channel, then it alerts you to sell your assets. It is the same case within the upturn trend. The channel mainly works well with patterns where if it is a downtrend, look for sell positions, and if it is an uptrend, look for buying positions.

If traders want to know the price changes based on time intervals, then they ought to apply the SMA, which means Simple Moving Average. This is a line drawn along the averages of the price movement at specific times. Let say a weekly time interval where it has seven days. It shows that action has taken place over the past seven days. Each average is obtained by the amount of trading divide day the time frame, which is seven. Therefore, in every consecutive mean, a line is plotted on the points, which is the SMA. SMAs with short ranges react more quickly than the ones with longer lengths. If you know that you easily identify the line and the point where you can access a profitable position, another case comes when you are using different portfolios. You will be forced to measure the SMA of the variable stocks. One may have a shorter SMA and the other a long one. In that particular state, when the short one closes against the long length, then it is an uptrend that prompts you to buy. If the vice versa happens, then it is a downtrend, which is a sell alarm.

Using the Moving Average Convergence/Divergence (MACD), you are likely to identify these opportunities within the swing trading. Remember that the MACD has two exponential averages: the signal line and the MACD points. These two indicate the position for the entry or the exit of the business. A bullish trend is realized if the MACD point crosses above the signal line that prompts you to enter the market. You need to sell your assets if the same line crosses below the signal point. That is an indicator of the bearish trend. Those professional traders know too well how to use this directional indicator. That is when the MACD is in the zero points that tell one that he or she is free to trade.

There is this crucial strategy called the Fibonacci retracement. It assists the trader in knowing the possible upturn of the stock turns. It is a behavior of swing trading that tends to affect most traders. It is also known as the stock reversal. That means you may be going on a good trend then abruptly an upturn happens. If you are not keen on this issue, you will make substantial losses. It happens even in unstable markets. Some news may say that a company is in the advent of selling its shares; so many subscribers will buy shares much. Then, what if the news changes by saying that the firm never reached an agreement on the shares transaction? Imagine the reversal pattern or upturn that would occur. How about the people who had staked all their accounts money, they would surely be hurting for their losses. This Fibonacci factor is built on the foundation that the securities typically retrace a particular portion before the reversal. Take an example you are given the Fibonacci's ratio like 23%, 40%, or 62%. These percentages tell of possible reversals. The 62% would be the resistance level and the limit 23% the support level. If the price movement bounces off the resistance level, then sell fast the assets with a profit before it bounces off the support point.

Countertrade is another strategy to use. It is a style that tries to catch the swing trade when it is in reversal. That is where there is an upturn of the swings. It also takes the trading on the current inverse market. It works similarly to the Fibonacci retracement on that this method tries to maximize the profit of the reversal time. It is a system that helps in risk management. When you are counter trading, you avoid the risk that results from an unstable market, which shows a sharp reversal in their direction. It also helps one amercing higher profits. That is because you know the point to sell or buy the stock or currency. There are also many returns from the reversal because the momentum of that curve is usually high. You can still use other portfolios and stocks that enable this behavior. You, therefore, maximize the diversification of the market. Therefore indicators like the MACD.RSI, Bollinger Bands are convenient to use in this scenario.

The forward-looking trading is also significant in ensuring promising returns. That means you anticipate that the trade will take a new direction. You forecast that there will be support and resistance shortly. This strategy works with conditional orders. This tactic requires an investor to use both the standard orders and options in coming upon with a practical value. These orders prompt the seller to articulate the selling price in the resistance points and the buying points in the support level. If you are forward-looking in those areas, you will minimize the risks and optimize the returns.

You should target making an accumulated profit that will go even for that period of weeks. This strategy works mainly for those people with patience. Many people mistake at this point because they are tempted by the returns they make. Imagine starting with a less penny, and then suddenly, you hit the jackpot. Then you would certainly feel you are a pro in this area. That perhaps is a lie to trap you in staking all your account money, which you will eventually lose. It is not a surprise that many cases have been reported concerning people blowing even the profits they had recently made. Always save that small profit you make over time. Let it accumulate, and you will realize how the size of the pocket is growing. If you are not in pressure to obtain much money, then you will be a crucial trader who can trace and spot profitable trends.

Have you ever gone on surfing? What interests you most in that activity? The most exciting part is the wave that comes and covers you. Then when you are swept by it, you try to surf hard so that another tide comes and covers you. Work with that strategy in the trading. When you identify a profitable point, Maximize on buying and selling in that area, and then exit the market. After some time, reenter the market and trade again as you keep coming out of the market. Have you have heard of guerrilla warfare. The monkey fights by hiding from its enemy, it then strikes then hides it again. Why don't you apply the same tactics? Keep on exiting the market after you have made a significant fortune, then reenter the market again and stake your amount. Before even any risk comes, you are already out. However, this scheme is not immune to the dangers, but it shortens any losses.

Sometimes, in this world, you reap benefits by going against the crowd. That is the resistance movement, which is the right stop to take. That does not mean if others are right, you ought to contradict them, or you start fighting the law because you read a segment that you go against the crowd. However, others may be wrong while you are light. Perhaps the market is programmed to disfavor the majority so that it can amerce their money. Then, you would be lucky if you are a minority group. In this case, you ought to trade against the momentum. This method works in the following ways:

- Trade into the resistance direction that utilizes the intense high while opposing the momentum change.
- If you are using the Japanese candles, check for the price rejection when the candle is in the downtrend.
- Draw your stop-loss above that peak point. Make sure that at this juncture, you trade narrowly on the next candle.
- Amerce any returns you suspect cohabiting on the nearest swing low.

If you are amateur in the business, you must know the market phrases. It might not sound a tactical switch but is fruitful in your trending. Even the expert knows that you cannot sell or buy without knowing the variables that are affecting the price movement. That is not about the indicators but is about the outside information that impacts the market. In every market, there are stages of peaks and recession periods. That is evident if you research on the historical trends. Therefore, if you anticipate a weak phase where there are fewer transactions, then go short on trading. If there is a high influx of shares or the market is promising trade massively. It makes you utilize and make many profits as soon as possible. Repeat the same cycle while exiting the weak phase and entering the strong one.

Always record everything in a journal or a book. This practice is done online, but make sure that each time you trade, get a pen and a paper. That makes you be organized in the trading. Record every move you make and your anticipated objective. Be on the look upon the technical analysis that you expect to use. Research how you will apply stock analysis in the market. Bookkeeping is a reference to how you will trade in the future. Records the deferent strategies which you have used and gauge them on the results they gave you. Adopt consistency in any approach you take. If you like to use the countertrade technique is consistence on it. Record also the risk management protocols you ought to apply. Such is the necessary stop losses. This date will even help you to establish other strategies. Engage an expert trader to assist you in trading. You will still realize that you are adapting to other trading tactics.

www.ingramcontent.com/pod-product-compliance
Lightning Source LLC
Chambersburg PA
CBHW071416210526
45465CB00001B/417